20.35

CAF|ICFM
THE FUNDRAISING SERIES

CORPORATE FUNDRAISING

EDITOR
VALERIE MORTON

1ST EDITION

ONE WEEK LOAN

D1428771

The fundraising series
Fundraising Strategy Redmond Mullin
Legacy Fundraising Sebastian Wilberforce (editor)
Trust Fundraising Anthony Clay (editor)

© 1999 Charities Aid Foundation and Institute of Charity Fundraising Managers

Published by:

Charities Aid Foundation
Kings Hill
West Malling
Kent
ME19 4TA

Tel +44 (0)1732 520000
Fax +44 (0)1732 520001
Web address http://www.charitynet.org
E-mail cafpubs@charitynet.org

Institute of Charity Fundraising Managers
Central Office
Market Towers
1 Nine Elms Lane
London
SW8 5NQ

Tel +44 (0)20 7627 3436
Fax +44 (0)20 7627 3508

Editor Andrew Steeds
Design and production GreenGate Publishing Services, Tonbridge
Printed and bound by Bell & Bain Ltd, Glasgow
Cover design Eugenie Dodd Typographics
A catalogue record for this book is available from the British Library
ISBN 1–85934–057–1

Contents

Appendices

The fundraising series

Fundraisers have always been among the most forward thinking in their willingness to share technique and experience. It is, therefore, surprising that, while books describing successful fundraising campaigns abound, no attempt has previously been made to establish an 'accepted body of literature' explaining fundraising activity as a whole within one series of volumes.

This is precisely what **The fundraising series** seeks to do.

Each volume is complete in itself, concentrating as it does on a key element within the fundraising 'marketing mix'. Taken together, the volumes that comprise this series will provide a comprehensive survey of existing fundraising practice, identifying analysing and explaining the breadth of fundraising experience currently available.

The titles in the series are not intended as fundraising manuals but as fundraising textbooks that identify and explain accepted fundraising practice within a coherent framework that may be easily translated back to the workplace. These 'working textbooks' are to be used by academics and practitioners alike. To this end, each title addresses the core fundraising competencies contained within the Certificate of Fundraising Management qualification awarded by the ICFM.

Each title explains the historical development of the fundraising practice in question and identifies the philosophical and theoretical context within which current work practice is grounded. The main body of each text is then devoted to an analysis of current activity and the identification of key learning points to guide future action.

Without a willing cohort of fundraising specialists prepared to share their skill and experience with others, this series would simply not have been possible. My thanks to each of them: together they have created the first, comprehensive series of fundraising textbooks anywhere in the world.

David Ford
Chairman, ICFM

About the authors

Sue Adkins

Before joining Business in the Community (BitC) in June 1995 to set up the Cause Related Marketing Campaign – which she now directs – Sue spent over 10 years in marketing, working as a marketing manager for InterCity (responsible for its business products), as an account director for Sampson Tyrrell, part of the WPP Group, and in other both business and agency consultancies.

Sue is recognised as an international expert in the area of Cause Related Marketing, has spoken all over the world and has written several reports and articles on the subject, including the first ever Cause Related Marketing guidelines and a book, *Cause Related Marketing – Who Cares Wins*, published by Butterworth Heinemann.

Manny Amadi

Manny Amadi MVO is managing director of Cause & Effect Marketing, the social marketing consultancy specialising in creating partnerships between the commercial and non-profit sectors.

Following an early career in the commercial sector, Manny held senior fundraising roles at the National Council of YMCAs and the seminal Prince's Youth Business Trust Big-Gift Appeal. He was, until 1998, Director of Development at the Prince's Trust, where he helped the Trust achieve and consolidate its status as the leading corporate fundraising charity.

Ian Anderson

Ian Anderson is Community Investment Director at Whitbread plc. Whitbread was one of the first companies to establish a dedicated Community Investment Programme in 1981 and has demonstrated its leadership in this field through pioneering initiatives such as YTS, Education Business Partnerships, Education Compacts, Employee Volunteering and, most recently, by making available for use by community organisations resources no longer needed by its various businesses. In 1998, Whitbread was recognised as Company of the Year in the BitC Awards for Excellence in Corporate Community Investment.

Ian has spent the last 13 years of his 35-year career with Whitbread managing its Community Programme. He is vice-chair of the National Centre for Volunteering and chair of REACH and is a director of the Corporate Responsibility Group. In the 1998 New Year's Honours he was awarded an OBE for services to volunteering.

Rachel Billsberry-Grass

Rachel Billsberry-Grass has several years' experience in the voluntary sector, including regional, events, trusts and corporate fundraising. She spent four years as Head of Corporate and Special Event Fundraising at the Muscular Dystrophy Group. Following a brief foray into the arts, she returned to the voluntary sector, working at Mencap, where she manages the corporate fundraising team.

Melanie Burfitt

Melanie Burfitt joined the Lymphoma Association as Head of Fundraising in 1996, with a brief to set up a national fundraising operation for the charity. She has succeeded in boosting income substantially and has created the Lymphoma Helpline Appeal. From an earlier career in marketing, Melanie moved to the voluntary sector in 1988 to join the NSPCC's corporate fundraising department, where she gained many years' experience developing and implementing corporate partnerships. Melanie is a founder and committee member of the Institute of Charity Fundraising Managers (ICFM) Chilterns group, and a regular trainer on the ICFM Corporate Fundraising course.

Andrew Craven

Andrew drifted into the charitable sector through a series of volunteer jobs, having graduated in Public Administration in the mid-1980s. His first paid job was with a small medical charity, National Eczema Society, where he was responsible for finance and membership. From the sponsorship experience gained there Andrew went on to become the Corporate Fundraising Manager for the British Red Cross, in which role he was deputed to build a corporate team capable of delivering all aspects of corporate fundraising and income from trusts and foundations, for projects both in the UK and overseas.

On his departure from the Red Cross, Andrew became the Development Director of the Natural History Museum. Here his main task is to increase annual income from more predictable income streams, although his current responsibilities are for all aspects of fundraising, with an emphasis on sponsorship for exhibitions and major gifts from individuals, trusts and foundations for capital projects.

Tony Elischer

Tony Elischer is director of Burnett Consulting UK. He has over 16 years' experience in the voluntary sector and, prior to his consultancy work, held several senior charity roles, including Head of Fundraising for Imperial Cancer Research Fund. He has extensive experience of helping charities around the world with strategy, fundraising, management and general trouble-shooting. He is an accomplished presenter, trainer and author.

Tony is a fellow of the UK's ICFM, a member of the ICFM executive and the National Fundraising Convention board and chair of the International Fundraising Workshop.

Jeremy Hughes

Jeremy Hughes is Director of Income Generation and Marketing at the British Red Cross. He has worked for campaigns, housing associations and charities, including NCH Action for Children, Muscular Dystrophy Group and Leonard Cheshire (where he led the charity's fundraising, marketing and communications teams), both in-house and as a consultant, over the past 20 years. He has served on the executive committee of the ICFM and as chairman of its Public Affairs Committee and co-chairman of the National Fundraisers Convention.

Karen Johnson

Karen Johnson is the Community Affairs Manager for Nationwide Building Society. She is responsible for Nationwide's community support programme of activities, including the relationship with Macmillan Cancer Relief and the Nationwide Awards for Voluntary Endeavour – a scheme to recognise people whose voluntary work has made a difference to their community.

Mike Lancaster

Mike Lancaster has worked at the Royal National Institute for the Blind (RNIB) for 10 years, as Director of External Relations, in which role he has overall responsibility for fundraising and public affairs. RNIB's fundraising has grown considerably in the 1990s under Mike's guidance, and has seen the development of corporate fundraising, legacy and donor marketing, as well as the emergence of new systems and approaches to community fundraising and volunteering.

Before joining RNIB, Mike worked for British Rail for nearly 20 years and held senior positions in advertising and marketing. He was the first marketing head for InterCity when it was set up as a stand-alone business in the mid-1980s.

Mike is active in ICFM as Honorary Treasurer and as a trustee of Cards for Good Causes and Contact a Family.

Stephen Lloyd

Stephen Lloyd is head of the charity department at Bates, Wells and Braithwaite, the leading Charity Law firm in the country. He is also trustee of a number of charities and author of the *Barclays Guide to Law for the Small Business* (1990) and *Charities Trading and the Law* (1995); he is co-author, with Fiona Middleton, of *The Charity's Acts Handbook* (1996) and a contributor to *Jordan's Charities Administration Service*. He is currently writing *Fundraising and the Law* for CAF. He lectures extensively on Charity Law.

Bert Moore

Bert Moore is the founder of purple;patch, a brand communications agency.

purple;patch works extensively in cause-related marketing with both charities (the Prince's Trust, NSPCC, MS Society) and corporations (BBC, Nike, Unilever) to devise issues-based strategies that benefit both brands. purple;patch pioneered the Prince's Trust's sports strategy, which combined the delivery of youth programmes through sport and raised over £1 million from sponsors, associations and government in its first year.

Prior to purple;patch, Bert ran the brand marketing group at Burson Marsteller, and before that he was with the management consultants, DDH.

Valerie Morton

Valerie Morton has been a successful fundraiser for over 21 years. She is one of the first 'career' fundraisers, having joined Help the Aged after gaining her Economics degree from Durham University. After a number of years in schools fundraising, she joined NSPCC to develop their Employee Fundraising initiatives and later to manage the Corporate Fundraising Department. More recent appointments include Head of Fundraising at the Outward Bound Trust and Head of National Fundraising at the Royal National Institute for the Blind.

Valerie is a long-standing and active member of ICFM, supporting a number of their committees and developing and running their Corporate Fundraising and Major Donor Fundraising training courses. She is now a freelance fundraiser and consultant, offering practical support and advice on a broad range of fundraising and management issues.

Hilary Partridge

Hilary Partridge was until recently Head of National Fundraising at the Royal National Institute for the Blind (RNIB), where she was responsible for managing a team fundraising from FTSE 100 companies, major grant-making trusts, the National Lottery and individuals, through direct appeals, legacy pledges and trading.

Hilary began her fundraising career at NSPCC, where she completed their graduate traineeship in fundraising and marketing before going on to work in legacy marketing. She joined RNIB as Legacy Marketing Manager, implementing their first-ever legacy marketing campaign before moving on to manage corporate fundraising, and from there to Head of National Fundraising. She is now a freelance fundraising consultant.

Brian Roberts-Wray

Brian Roberts-Wray enjoyed a 30-year career in the corporate sector (principally in the marketing discipline in Unilever) before joining the voluntary sector as Director of Fundraising at Marie Curie Cancer Care in 1989, where he remained until 1995. During that time, Marie Curie's voluntary income grew from £15 million to £37 million. On leaving Marie Curie, Brian became a consultant in voluntary sector management, where he specialises in fundraising strategy development.

He joined the ICFM in 1990, became a member of Services Committee in 1992, was elected to the Executive Committee in 1993, served as Vice-Chairman 1994–96 and as Chairman 1996–98. In 1998 he was elected a fellow of the ICFM.

Jon Scourse

Jon Scourse switched his career from industry to the voluntary sector in 1993 when he joined Feed the Children, now Children's Aid Direct. Initially Head of Corporate Fundraising, he developed company support with special emphasis on Gifts in Kind. This was based on identifying opportunities for companies to recycle their products so as to benefit directly those in need, especially in Eastern Europe. At its peak, the value of such support was worth over £2 million annually. Jon has additionally developed substantial new income from corporate challenge events. He is currently National Fundraising Manager for the Guide Dogs for the Blind Association.

Stephen Serpell

Stephen Serpell is head of BT's Community Partnership Programme. At £15 million, this is one of the largest community programmes in the UK, while

BT's overall contribution to the community totals nearly £28 million. In 1999's Business in the Community Awards for Excellence, BT received the overall award for Impact on Society from the Prime Minister.

Stephen was previously a Board Member in BT's Managed Network Services, where he was in charge of BT's Data Services and was responsible for a substantial revenue and profit line. In other roles, he has led business and strategic planning teams, and founded and directed a consultancy, as well as being involved in external work in the community.

Introduction and acknowledgements

Valerie Morton

What is corporate fundraising?

It is very easy to assume that there is a simple answer to the question, 'What is corporate fundraising?'. The obvious one is that it is raising money from the corporate sector. Given how this fundraising discipline has developed over the last 15 years or so, however, the answer is anything but simple, and for a number of reasons:

- Money is not the only support that companies give to charities. As illustrated in Chapters 13 and 15, there are now some inspiring examples of how both companies and charities have developed the area of in-kind support, whether this is through the secondment of staff, facilitating staff volunteering, or donating goods or services.
- The term 'fundraising' carries the connotation that there is an element at least of philanthropy involved. The continuing rise of cause-related marketing initiatives, which require the achievement of clear commercial objectives, brings this idea into question.
- Largely as a result of the two previous points, a number of charities have now introduced new descriptions for this area of work. Examples include corporate marketing, financial development and commercial relations.
- Many corporate fundraisers do not confine themselves to generating income from commercial organisations. With the onset of employee fundraising initiatives, for example, and of payroll giving in particular, their remit includes bodies that have employees such as government departments, hospitals and even charities.

To provide a framework for the scope of this book, a suggested textbook definition of the term corporate fundraising would be: the generation of financial or in-kind support from a commercial or non-commercial organisation, and its associated stakeholders, where their relationship with the organisation is instrumental in initiating the support.

The corporate fundraising marketplace

Statistics from Charities Aid Foundation (CAF) give the value of support to the voluntary sector from the 'top' 500 corporate donors as £305.6 million in 1996–97 (Pharoah, 1998). Although this figure is encouraging in its own right, the full picture is even brighter. Even with the best recording systems, it is unlikely that every single piece of in-kind support is recorded (among many possible examples, witness the number of companies who let charities use rooms occasionally for meetings, or who will use their resources to bind a proposal document for a charity, or who will pass over left-over stocks). It is also unlikely that every pound of income generated by volunteering employees is captured in the statistics.

There is also the issue of corporate trusts or foundations. Technically, these operate independently of companies, but they are funded, initially or on a continuing basis, from corporate funds. Corporate foundations that are members of the Association of Charitable Foundations (ACF) had an income of over £99 million in 1997–98, according to the ACF's annual report for that year.

Finally, consider the income of over £24 million a year generated through donations from individuals through the payroll-giving scheme (Byers, 1998): although matched donations from companies will be included in the figure of £305.6 million given above, payroll donations from individuals are not, and yet they are made possible only through the role of the company in deducting donations from pay at source.

Providing statistics on the size of the corporate fundraising market can give the impression that this is the value of support for which all corporate fundraisers are competing. Experience shows that fundraisers who are able to inject an element of creativity into their work have the potential to unleash additional support from hitherto untapped corporate budgets. Examples might include companies facilitating the distribution of 'stick pins' that generate donations to the charity, the use of training budgets to pay for teams of staff to enter 'challenge' events that benefit charities through sponsorship or the use of corporate hospitality budgets to pay for tickets to a charity event.

The good news is that, as usual, statistics tell only half of the story. Corporate fundraisers have a vast and wide-ranging market place in which to operate, which represents an exciting challenge for any fundraiser and offers huge potential, provided they apply creativity and good practice.

The role of corporate fundraising within the charity

Corporate fundraising is often seen as the golden egg of fundraising – whether this is because of the perceived excitement of dealing with the corporate sector, the chance of being invited to glamorous functions or simply the enjoyment of being involved in such a creative area is unclear. However, as Chapter 3 indicates, success in this area depends not only on the fundraiser concerned, but also on a wide variety of other people involved in a charity, all of whom need to be aware of the expectations placed upon charities working in partnerships with companies.

Whereas other fundraising disciplines may be seen as simply ways to raise money, corporate fundraising has the potential to have both a positive and a negative impact on a number of aspects of the charity. If this is recognised at chief-executive level, the impact can be substantial.

The positive impact includes:

- the opportunity, even for small charities, to raise relatively large sums of money – the increasing acceptance of employee fundraising in particular raised the ceiling of corporate support;
- cost ratios for an established corporate-fundraising function are usually substantially better than for most other areas of fundraising. The latest FUNDRATIO statistics from the Centre for Interfirm Comparison show corporate fundraising raising on average £4.06 per £1 spent, a figure above other areas such as direct marketing, local house-to-house fundraising and local fundraising;
- corporate bodies with a retail focus can offer unrivalled access to the public, which, for charities, represents a currently underused way of promoting their key messages;
- companies are often the target audience for a charity's policy messages – whether it is an environmental charity seeking to promote sustainable development, or a charity representing disabled people whose objective is to influence employment practice.

Examples of the negative impact may be:

- where financial support by a company is conditional on a matter that may not be in keeping with the charity's strategy – for example, where a request is made for the money to be used in a geographical area that the charity does not feel to be a priority;
- where actions by the company affect the charity, as a result of their partnership – for example where a company supporting a children's charity launches a new child-related product of which the charity disapproves.

These, and other, matters are addressed and illustrated in Chapters 7 and 12, which are concerned with the ethical issues of corporate fundraising.

A responsibility to the sector as a whole

The vast majority of corporate fundraisers, or charity personnel who have corporate fundraising as part of their role, operate on a totally professional basis and are excellent ambassadors for the sector.

On a number of occasions in the past, however, the actions of individual fundraisers have had an effect on the sector as a whole. Some years ago, a major high-street name approached a large number of charities to see whether they would like to benefit from a Christmas promotion. The company wanted to gain from association with the high-profile charity names, but was only prepared to offer a tiny sum of money to each charity. Most charities turned down the offer, on the basis that the company would be getting a benefit disproportionate to the money on offer. One charity, however, agreed, believing that any money was worth having. As a result, the company felt negative about working with the voluntary sector. Had all the charities taken the same, reasoned, approach, it may have been possible to influence the company and ultimately benefit the sector as a whole.

Similar situations have arisen where a charity has either made commitments it is unlikely to be able to fulfil, or has simply not fulfilled pledges, as illustrated in Chapter 12. This reduces the prospect of the companies involved working with charities in the future.

Any charity personnel working with the corporate sector has a responsibility to the voluntary sector as a whole to ensure the operation of best practice at all times. What constitutes that best practice is an area of continuous discussion in the sector. Chapters 3, 4 and 5 provide some useful insights into the management of the corporate fundraising function from experienced professionals, while the case histories of successful corporate partnerships in Chapters 9, 10 and 11 show what can be achieved when best practice is followed.

Any successful partnership depends equally on the parties involved. The case histories from the corporate sector in Chapters 14, 15 and 16 make valuable reading for any corporate fundraising professional.

Corporate fundraising has evolved rapidly over the last twelve years, which is the length of time that the book editor has been involved in the field. The challenge for all corporate fundraisers now is to take the lessons from the past and ensure that future partnership really do offer value for money for all concerned.

About this book

This book is divided into three broad sections, the first of which provides a theoretical and practical context to the remaining contributions. Section 2 uses a number of actual case studies – not all of them successful – to illustrate many of the points made in the first section, from the charity's perspective. Section 3 considers corporate–charity partnerships from the company's perspective, again illustrating the discussion with reference to real case-study material. Finally, following a concluding chapter, the Appendices feature a list of useful contacts and bibliographical material, together with an important chapter on the legal and tax issues surrounding corporate fundraising.

Books are not written and produced overnight, so much of the case-study material gathered here will be at least a year old by the time the book is published. However, the book editor and authors are satisfied that the points illustrated in these case studies are by no means time-specific, and that the studies themselves have an enduring relevance and serve as valuable examples of the best practice of corporate fundraising.

Editor's acknowledgements

This book has been made possible only by the generous support, in time, knowledge and expertise, of the authors and editors involved.

My special thanks go to each of the chapter authors, for providing their own individual insights into the vast and complex subject of corporate fundraising. I am delighted that such experienced and respected fundraisers felt able to support this book and to offer such valuable contributions.

When in his position of Chief Executive of ICFM, Stephen Lee provided invaluable support, advice and inspiration, for which I am particularly grateful.

I owe a great debt to the desk editor of this book, Andrew Steeds, whose specialist, and enviable, skills ensured a highly professional publication, and whose good humour enabled me to keep my sanity while facing the challenge of putting the book together.

My thanks go to CAF and ICFM, who had the foresight to conceive this **Fundraising series**, and who entrusted me with the compilation of this book.

On a personal level, I could not have completed this book without the unfailing commitment of my husband, Adrian Penrose, and the impeccable timing of my son, Leo Penrose, who synchronised his arrival in the world perfectly with the writing and publication schedule of this book.

PART ONE

Background and best practice

CHAPTER ONE

Historical context and current environment

Tony Elischer

Corporate support of charities – the roots and origins

The distribution of corporate wealth to charitable endeavour and public bene-fit mirrors the development of the voluntary sector through history. The United Kingdom is unique in the uninterrupted passage of prosperous trade over many centuries. From the earliest times, there is evidence of both indi-vidual and corporate philanthropy based on the fruits of that trade being used to support philanthropic activity.

Mercantile and corporate wealth played a significant part in the development of the physical structures of community and civic life between 1480 and 1660. During this period, corporate benefaction led the way in 'the building of town halls, the provision of corporate plate, endowments to secure the lessening of tax burdens, and a great variety of other gifts designed to make divers com-munities more attractive and agreeable places in which to work and live.'

In other ways, too, corporate and mercantile wealth, laced with a healthy regard for commercial self-interest, served to promote substantive corporate benefaction and fashion modern society. Even in these early times, the moti-vation behind corporate support was complex and sophisticated, ranging from pure philanthropic ideal, through ambitious desire for self-promotion and social aggrandisement, to recognition of mutual commercial self-interest.

The presence of local, regional and national corporate support contributed to the success of a wide range of charitable endeavour in the eighteenth and nine-teenth centuries. Both in the United Kingdom and also across Europe, wealthy merchants used their own wealth and that of their companies to promote the establishment of a civic and ecumenical infrastructure that the state still regarded as beyond its compass.

As today, London played a leading part. The formation of the City of London around the great livery companies was based on companies' realisation that they would need to provide for more than just individual or corporate wealth if their commercial enterprise was to be maintained and expanded. Throughout subsequent history, City livery companies and the corporate benefaction that supports their work have been hugely influential in the creation of infrastructures, the development of social rehabilitation, and the concerted support for health, education and the alleviation of poverty.

A number of authors have charted the extraordinary impact of the City institutions on the development of philanthropy from the 1600s to the modern era, providing a comprehensive summary of highly sophisticated company-giving schemes around the same period. Their findings clearly demonstrate that debate over appropriate levels of corporate philanthropic support as opposed to commercial sponsorship is by no means purely a modern-day phenomenon.

By the late 1800s, there was sufficient public disquiet about the corporate-giving policies of these companies to promote a Royal Commission to examine (among other things) the nature of corporate-giving programmes, the moral imperative towards philanthropic endeavour that corporate profit demands and the ambiguous nature of philanthropic endeavour when it is inexplicably intertwined with commercial benefit. Many of the arguments paraded in the 1880s rehearse the debates over corporate giving that continue to the present day.

The development of corporate fundraising in the nineteenth century

The origins of what today is classified as corporate fundraising are to be found in the nineteenth century. The abundance of commercial opportunity grounded in the birth of the industrial revolution; commercial advantage, developed through centuries of unrestricted trade; the ease of access to cheap sources of raw material and markets delivered by colonial rule – all conspired to encourage a leap in privately owned corporate wealth at the turn of the nineteenth century. The works and policies of great industrialists of the time, like Cadbury, Wedgwood and Rowntree, pioneered the idea of investing in employees and their local communities.

Much of the force behind this explosion in corporate philanthropy was profoundly personal and often idiosyncratic in nature. The majority of the great reforming corporate institutions were privately owned, family dynasties, themselves highly regimented and controlled through the strict hierarchy of family lineage. Of equal importance was the impact that religious belief played in providing an ideological framework within which corporate philanthropy became an important moral imperative. These great industrial barons were often hard pressed to distinguish between private, family, religious and corporate affiliation. The social and moral condition of employees and their families, the values of the family itself, were intricately intertwined with the fortunes of the company and the advancement of wealth and personal esteem.

There are important lessons for the modern-day corporate fundraiser to take from this complexity, not least in answer to the question, 'Just what is the degree of philanthropic endeavour that might truly be regarded as "corporate" in nature?' Was the development of corporate giving in the Victorian period truly corporate in nature, or was it more importantly grounded in individual philanthropic intent?

Formalisation of corporate fundraising as an activity

Charity and corporate activity have been transformed in the latter part of the twentieth century. Before 1945, both sectors continued to develop organically, working on the long unbroken, mutually compatible traditions of free trade and corporate beneficence.

There is an inextricable connection between corporate philanthropy and individual giving because so much individual wealth is the result of commercial success. Much of the product of corporate wealth destined to further philanthropic endeavour was actively channelled into the endowment of large grant-making trusts, or provided by large benefaction to particular service-provision charities that took little active part in soliciting the funds they received.

Some significant pro-active corporate fundraising practice did emerge successfully in this period, most notably the development of post-tax employee-giving schemes by Barnardo's. In truth, however, the main impetus behind corporate support continued to be vested in the self-enlightened practice of particular employers, as industrialists recognised the value of community support to their business operations and objectives.

From the end of World War II the respective positions of the corporate and charitable sector have become far more stylised with regard to corporate fundraising. Although privately owned corporate philanthropy remains important in its contribution to corporate fundraising, today it has been matched, if not surpassed, by the post-war growth of publicly owned corporate giving.

As companies have grown larger and more complex, as departmental functionalism within companies provides opportunity for a breadth of competing ideology in the same organisation, as different forms of corporate ownership and structure determine differing corporate outputs, so fundraising success has grown more and more to depend on an understanding of the various motivations behind different types of corporate giving.

The rise of marketing and advertising as pivotal disciplines in corporate enterprise has provided new and potentially lucrative sources of corporate support to the charitable sector. At the same time, they have brought the corporate community itself to a deeper understanding of its own, often complex and differing motivations behind various types of support for the charitable sector.

As far as the voluntary sector is concerned, access to new technology, the drive towards corporate public ownership and the development of a more transparent, stakeholder concept of corporate governance, has provided it with greater understanding of corporate giving than ever before. Ease of access to this greater knowledge has spurned ever-greater competition for the corporate pound. In turn, this has forced both the corporate and charitable sectors to become more disciplined and professional in the manner in which they address corporate giving.

The position now

Today, corporate fundraising has become an essential component in the broader fundraising strategy of the majority of charities. Corporate fundraisers manage their own complex marketing mix, ranging from philanthropic support through sponsorship, event management, corporate adoption schemes, social investment programmes, cause-related marketing, affinity marketing, franchising, employee fundraising, gifts in kind and secondment.

For their part, the major companies have reviewed their support of the charitable sector against far more rigorous benchmarked criteria. Proactive strategies of corporate support, outlining precisely how companies will support the sector, have been developed and implemented with a growing willingness by a wide range of companies.

Greater competition, greater understanding of their own role and required outputs from support of the charitable sector on the part of companies have led to a more complex and sophisticated environment for corporate giving. To succeed, only the creative and skilful need apply; only those with a clear understanding of the complex motivations behind corporate support developed through centuries of practice are likely to fulfil their objectives. It is to this understanding of the company that the next chapter turns.

CHAPTER TWO

The company as a resource

Tony Elischer

Introduction

Fundraisers considering companies as resources need to think in the widest possible terms about the many different ways that companies can support a charity. Companies consist of three basic elements: people, budgets and resources. Fundraisers are used to working with people, as people give to people first; all they need to appreciate is that people in companies are given budgets and resources to achieve set objectives that contribute to the profit of a company. Companies are simply bodies of people combined for commercial purposes to make a profit from a commercial activity. If fundraisers accept this and adopt a positive attitude towards this activity, then they can begin to open their eyes to how they might link into many of the opportunities that companies offer.

Figure 1 seeks to define a typical range of people, budgets and resources that might be found in a company and to list a typical range of benefits that a charity might offer a company. Too many charities limit their approaches by thinking simply of the chair, marketing director and the charity committee. Yet there are many more access points and potential areas from which to generate support.

The focus is all too often on money, rather than thinking through the full spectrum of charitable giving: time, money and goods. As this area becomes more competitive, it is essential to think more creatively and to find more unique ways of working with companies. It is also necessary to think about a relationship and how to start and develop it rather than always aspiring to the top and the highest value forms of support.

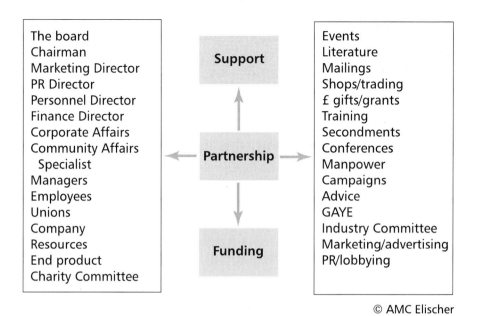

	Support	Events
The board		Literature
Chairman		Mailings
Marketing Director		Shops/trading
PR Director		£ gifts/grants
Personnel Director		Training
Finance Director		Secondments
Corporate Affairs		Conferences
Community Affairs	← Partnership →	Manpower
Specialist		Campaigns
Managers		Advice
Employees		GAYE
Unions		Industry Committee
Company		Marketing/advertising
Resources	Funding	PR/lobbying
End product		
Charity Committee		

© AMC Elischer

Figure 1 How the people in a company may benefit a charity

The key players in a company

At the top of most companies is the **board**, the body of people who represent the shareholders' interests and generally serve to keep the company on track and operating at an acceptable profit level. This group is often a considerable size with people drawn from all walks of life, many of whom may already be known to a charity through the contacts of its trustees and board. The value of these contacts is their ability to advise, guide and facilitate introductions to different staff and departments within their company. Many directors also serve on more than one board, so cultivation is the key in this area.

Under the board is the chair, **chief executive** or **managing director** (depending on the size and organisational format of the company), the key person who leads and guides the company. As the most powerful person, they are well targeted by charities for support of varying kinds, and many of them have developed sophisticated defence shields as a result.

Historically, this person was seen as the key to philanthropic funds and general influence within the company. Now, although the influence remains, in many cases the funds have been allocated to specialists or to other budgets where corporate objectives can be achieved through their deployment. As in the case of the board, the main gift this person can give is their interest in and endorsement of your cause, leading to advice and guidance on how to work with companies in general.

Of the directors that are responsible to the chair, and who represent the key functions within a company, **marketing** has to be the top prospect. Charities appear to think that marketing directors have lots of money, which they do, but for very tightly defined purposes. The starting place here must be to understand that marketing is 'the process responsible for identifying, satisfying and anticipating customer requirements profitably'. Marketing is the heart of a company, and any charity that chooses to target it with a proposition or request should ask itself how that proposition is helping to fulfil marketing's role for the company. This is the commercial end of seeking corporate support, where sponsorship and cause-related marketing are key. As other chapters will illustrate, the rewards are high, but so are the levels of competition and the technical skill required to work effectively in this area.

Charities invest considerable resources in targeting marketing departments for sales promotions or cause-related marketing opportunities. In general, these approaches are unsuccessful. Companies will decide themselves when these types of activities are appropriate and they will then seek suitable partners. Charities aiming to be successful in this area should concentrate on building a reputation for working effectively with companies and on developing their brand awareness in the market place. This way they will find themselves on company shortlists for opportunities. Only an exceptional idea will truly succeed from cold in this area: to introduce ideas and achieve a hearing, existing relationships are the key.

The main departments

Public relations (PR) is a useful point of contact for charities for several reasons, most obviously because this department acts as the interface between a company and the public and may therefore be a good place for information, views and guidance.

Until the advent of payroll giving, no one really paid much attention to the **personnel**, or **human resources** (HR) department, and they were relatively easy to gain access to and befriend. This is no longer necessarily the case, as charities are seen to be after one thing only: access to employees to promote payroll schemes. Charities need to exercise lateral thinking in this important area, as HR is a real key to company networks and employees.

HR departments purchase and plan training for employees. Many of these training places go to waste each year through sickness and changes in plans. A charity registering an interest in such opportunities can often be contacted at short notice and offered places on sales, presentation or management courses for its staff or volunteers. Indeed, some companies now run extra courses just to offer to the voluntary sector. Volunteering and secondment are two further areas for consideration here.

Corporate affairs is often the silent function within major companies, the role of which can vary from handling relationships with government, to co-ordinating planning, to defining and protecting the company image or brand, or even preparing crisis PR strategies. Any of these areas is at a high level of operation that usually involves reporting to the chair and certainly plays a major role in guiding the company and its activities.

Finance, sales and other directors in a company, and their functions, can be analysed in this way, but the key point is that each position and function within a company has the potential to offer opportunities. It is a matter of thinking outside conventional wisdom to find an appropriate approach that may help a charity stand out from the crowd.

One other area worth noting in relation to the key people and functions is any **specialist functions** a company may have that could either have a particular affinity with your cause or be of specialist interest. For example, charities working in medical research may find a link with company medical officers a useful way into a company, and charities for children may find links with crèche managers appropriate. Legal officers, economists or IT specialists may offer specific skills to charities at a particular stage of their development.

Employees, resources and other agencies

Under these main functions you have an army of **employees** who all offer the potential to introduce a charity to the workplace and to their company. Too few charities take the trouble to introduce corporate fundraising to their donors and volunteers through newsletters and mailings. Simply highlighting the value of the area and asking for contacts or interest in helping to develop programmes may provide useful leads. Companies are devolving more power and decisions to employees, particularly in the area of charity and community involvement. Charities need to respond to this by working both at head office and at grassroots level.

Beyond people there are **resources**, a major area of opportunity often over-looked in the UK, or certainly seen as a secondary option for support. Yet this is an area where it is often easier to get a gift, and for the company to give, since a gift of resources does not necessarily mean money off the bottom line. A brainstorm around this area will lead to many different options:

- gift of end-product for use, resale or as a prize
- use of empty buildings for office space
- use of corporate buildings for meetings or events
- photocopying and printing facilities
- stationery supplies
- old office equipment: furniture, computers, etc.

As in the USA, there are now specialist UK charities that encourage these gifts, promote their value and act as a clearing-house for companies who want to find recipients. A well thought-out programme will bring the benefit of another way of linking with companies.

Any review of companies would not be complete without highlighting the many **auxiliary agencies** that companies are increasingly using to fulfil specific roles: advertising, PR, sponsorship, recruitment, sales promotion, etc. These agencies offer another way into companies; more importantly, they offer a filter for ideas. Many of these agencies are retained to solve problems, create opportunities and basically to have good ideas on behalf of the company. Befriending them can provide an invaluable opportunity to 'test' your ideas and to seek guidance on refinement and more appropriate targeting. Charities should also strive to achieve awareness of their organisation, its activities and interest in working with the corporate sector through this group.

At the base of the 'company as a resource' model is the traditional **charity committee**, which will distribute the donations budget that many companies still have. The demands on these funds inevitably mean that exceptional skills are needed if a case is to succeed. A charity must also be prepared to accept the 'lottery' element of the distribution of these funds. Despite this, it is almost essential that charities approach these committees if they are to build profile and to seek funding in return for minimal requirements. As with PR, charity committees can be a friend to the charity sector, offering guidance and advice, but charities should be clear about their strategy before making approaches and recognise that the creative approaches required to gain access to marketing budgets do not necessarily apply here.

This account of the typical people, budgets and resources to be found within companies demonstrates the wide range of opportunities available and illustrates why every charity should have corporate support in their funding portfolio. The secret is to set a strategy and to attempt a different approach from that made by the other 180,000 charities that have targeted companies as a potentially wealthy source of donations.

This model applies in full only to larger companies, although many of the ideas and elements will still apply to medium-sized, regionally based companies. Research will indicate which companies follow this model and where you need to make suitable adjustments to the model and its thinking. Rather than starting with national companies – which is what everyone tends to do – it would be easier to start with the hundreds of thousands of local and regional companies that rarely receive imaginative professional approaches for their support.

The right hand side of Figure 1 illustrates some of the needs and opportunities a typical charity may have in relation to companies. Each charity needs to lay out its own 'market stall' before approaching companies, in order to draw up a priority and take a flexible approach when seeking partnerships with companies. Cold approaches are becoming increasingly difficult, especially when the first approach is for money. Charities need to consider how they can start a dialogue and how to build it over time as confidence and credibility build.

The overall perspective

In recent years corporate fundraising has undergone a shift in emphasis. There has been a move away from the technique whereby specific roles were allocated in corporate fundraising teams to a more generalist function with a limited client portfolio. Figure 2 illustrates this structure and highlights the importance of the individual, who is at the centre and must possess an understanding and overview of all the components.

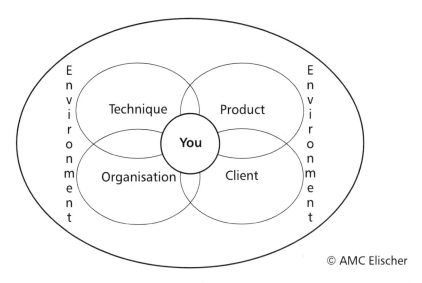

© AMC Elischer

Figure 2 The five elements of corporate fundraising

The five elements identified within the environment are the headings under which all elements of the corporate fundraising process fit. The division within this model helps to group and analyse all the elements; it also serves to highlight the variables in this activity that the fundraiser controls.

You

The individual is the driving force behind any fundraising. You need to understand and appreciate how the corporate sector works and, from these core skills, to review your attitude towards your product and the task of selling it to companies. It is the job of the corporate fundraiser to identify projects within their organisation that have the potential to attract the different forms of corporate support, and then to package them in the appropriate way. This process is an integral part of developing belief and ownership in the fundraiser. In commercial selling, 'the first sale we have to make is to ourselves'. It is hard to convey enthusiasm, particularly through the written word, but belief comes through time and time again.

Corporate fundraising is high-energy fundraising and fiercely competitive. In addition to the unique selling points (USPs) of the project and the charity, energy, belief and commitment can play a major part – after all, people 'give to people first, whatever else second'. Many charities exclude corporate opportunities because they believe that they have an unpopular cause that lacks 'sex appeal'; such charities are disadvantaging themselves before they start. Virtually every charitable cause can gain some sort of corporate support, providing the fundraiser has a positive mental attitude. Corporate fundraising demands dedication, passion and commitment, arguably beyond any other fundraising technique.

Product

Many charities still operate with a piecemeal set of projects, often inflicted on the corporate fundraiser as the things for which other departments and people would like funding or support. You will need to organise a thorough audit of your charity and develop a full portfolio of projects that form your core products in the market place if you are to succeed. People often do not realise the dual battles corporate fundraisers must face in not only marketing their portfolios, but also establishing them in the first place. This technique often involves 'selling' the name of the organisation and aligning its values with those of a commercial company, so it is important to gain approval and commitment at all levels of a charity. Think of your corporate fundraising department or activity as a shop that needs stocking with products attractive to consumers. Like a shop you should try new products but, just as importantly, you should not take up valuable shelf space stocking products that clearly are not going to sell.

Try to identify projects that help companies to 'reach the unreachable'; profile your audiences; think creatively around the people of influence to whom you have access and develop a list of celebrity supporters.

As consumers we expect quality and service in our transactions with companies, yet in the corporate fundraising area we do not do enough to ensure that the same attributes apply to our activities. Consider every aspect of your product and the way you market and deliver it; strive for the highest level of quality, and refuse to settle for second best, just because you are a charity. People's expectations of service increase each year, and more and more companies fail to deliver in this area; for their own reputation and survival, and that of the sector as a whole, charities have to deliver.

Technique

There are many and varied techniques within corporate fundraising, at the core of which there are a number of essential techniques that charities wishing to exploit and explore the potential of corporate support must master. The challenge for fundraisers is to extend, develop and refine these techniques to make them offer more for both the charity and the company. The key elements of sponsorship do not vary, but success depends on how people translate and use these elements. The textbook and training course are vital to understanding, but adapting and learning from experience are more important. Success with techniques means not being hung up about them, viewing them as instruments to be used rather than rules to be obeyed.

The key skill in all areas of corporate fundraising is the ability to put yourself in the place of the person you are approaching, to get into their mind and circumstances. Experience and awareness provide the ability to identify the correct motivator to use. What is the trigger to get the contact in the company to say 'Yes'? Motivators are governed by the mind and the heart: the mind reviews the logic, business benefits and general appropriateness; the heart reviews the cause, its need and emotional appeal.

The foundations of a good approach are built upon research, but applying imagination and creativity to a technique are two other 'converters' that will distinguish your approach from others. Capturing your prospect's imagination is an important part of your approach.

Client

Most people will have experienced the courting process. Corporate fundraisers should use this experience and begin to view their approaches to companies as individual courting experiences. They should see these approaches in terms of building relationships, promoting understanding and mutual respect, and agreeing to partnerships where both parties are comfortable and content with their part of the agreement – all in the recognition that different relationships require different timings, approaches and energy levels.

There is an old adage that it is ten times more difficult to acquire a new client than it is to retain and upgrade an existing one, and yet the drive of much corporate activity is to acquire new clients to meet the needs of new projects. Why? Just like a consumer purchasing any item, if clients are happy with the product and service they receive they are likely to return for more or at least to be receptive to further approaches and propositions. This highlights the need to build a true partnership to enable you to look on clients as a return on your investment. By making past corporate partners friends of the charity there is not only a greater possibility of further joint projects but also the opportunity to ask for introductions and recommendations to other key prospects you have identified.

Organisation

Organisation is the area most frequently neglected by the corporate fundraiser. The corporate fundraising mix is so wide that most organisations will find a technique that is right for them and their available resources. Resources are the key word: a corporate fundraiser must define precisely what investment the organisation is prepared to commit to this area, since this will influence their choice of technique as much as the work of the organisation.

The ethical issues surrounding corporate fundraising should be reviewed under this heading. These issues will vary for each organisation, and it is important to set a policy that is right for the individual needs of the organisation: are there areas of commerce and industry with which the organisation does not feel compatible or with which it would not feel comfortable aligning itself? The important thing is to agree the policy before any corporate approaches or negotiations are instigated.

Corporate alertness

Any corporate fundraising function should promote 'corporate alertness' within their organisation and encourage staff to pick up on any corporate contact either made by the company or made by anyone associated with the charity, from trustees to directors to volunteers and donors. Organisations often miss the contacts that are under their noses; make sure every part of the organisation is aware of the importance of companies and any contacts that exist with them.

The model presented in Figure 2 should be used as a flexible framework to encourage fundraisers in the corporate area to consider the principal component parts that will lead to success. New ideas, experience and environment changes should be integrated into the circles as they occur, making it an ever-evolving structure for fundraising development and achievement.

CHAPTER THREE

Managing corporate fundraising

Melanie Burfitt

Introduction

Companies' support of the community – known as Corporate Community Involvement (CCI) – is today more formal and often more commercial than it used to be. The essence of the activity is partnership, and the charity that meets the objectives of the company most closely is the one most likely to receive its support.

The management of the relationship between companies and charities requires specialist skills. In medium-sized to larger charities, such fundraising is likely to be the responsibility of a corporate fundraising section which may have any-thing from one to thirty staff. In a smaller charity, this function may be integrated into the responsibilities of the sole fundraiser or the chief executive.

Either way, particular attention needs to be paid to the way in which a charity approaches, negotiates with and manages partnerships with a commercial company: this chapter provides some indication of how to organise that activity.

The role and scope of corporate fundraising

What is corporate fundraising, and how does it work?

Companies support charities in a variety of ways, some of which give the company measurable commercial benefits. Indeed, it has become common practice for companies to seek partnerships that offer tangible benefits to themselves – such as publicity, enhanced image, goodwill with staff, cus-tomers and suppliers – as well as providing funds and awareness for the charity.

The previous chapter explained in detail the role of the company as a resource. Broadly speaking, this role may be characterised as four different ways in which companies may provide support to charities.

1 Philanthropic giving

Many companies uphold the tradition of disinterested philanthropy and give donations to charities with 'no strings attached'; some have corporate trusts or foundations specifically set up as a means of providing community support efficiently and tax effectively. A corporate strategy and an annual budget for charitable support are now commonplace, particularly among the larger companies. It is not uncommon for staff to have an active role in the distribution of donations, either through recommendations or through a staff charity committee.

In the current climate, where commercial partnerships between companies and charities are increasingly high profile, this important and potentially valuable area of support can sometimes be overlooked.

2 Cause-related marketing

A company may use its marketing budget for a promotion or a sponsorship linked to a cause. Such activity may involve, for example, sponsorship of a charity event, project or publication. The key criterion for such activity is that it meets the company's marketing objectives, which may be launching a new product or service, or increasing the uptake of such products or services.

Companies undertaking cause-related marketing will also be seeking a return on their investment: their objective is to take advantage of the charity's positive image in order to enhance their own image, create goodwill, and build loyalty with their customers. For a cause-related activity to achieve maximum success, there needs to be synergy between the company and the charity, either because the product area is relevant or because there is a shared target audience.

Cause-related marketing can raise substantial funds for charities, but it tends to be only charities with a high, and clearly defined, profile that are approached by companies. Charities need to be aware that cause-related marketing, and charity promotions in particular, is a specialist area, and the legality of ideas should be carefully checked by an expert. Pro-actively targeting companies for joint promotions can be very labour intensive; for this reason, many charities are reactive rather than proactive in this area of fundraising (see Chapters 6 and 11 for a more detailed analysis of cause-related marketing).

3 Employee support

The third potential source of income from a company is through its employees. This may involve companies adopting a particular cause as their Charity of the Year (as Tesco, for example, adopted the Muscular Dystrophy Group in 1996 – see Chapter 9). A fundraising challenge is issued to staff, with money raised often being matched by the company, in part or in full, and corporate events scheduled throughout the adoption period to raise additional funds. A more recent trend is for adoptions to be for either a shorter period (eg a two-week 'blitz') or longer term, particularly if there is also a cause-related marketing element to the adoption.

A formal adoption can be a major opportunity for a charity with the resources and staff to take advantage of it. For the company, such an activity can boost staff morale, and encourage team building and the development of staff skills. It can generate useful publicity, particularly locally, give the company a higher profile within the community, and help recruit and retain staff.

It is, however, important to note that being chosen as a 'Charity of the Year' will cause a sudden increase in annual income for the adopted charity which it will not necessarily be possible to sustain in subsequent years.

Fundraising within a company is sometimes carried out less formally by a core group of active fundraisers, often operating on an *ad-hoc* basis but sometimes as a formal committee. Identifying and building a relationship with these people can be an excellent way into a company, particularly for smaller charities or those with less popular causes. Charities with members or clients should also look at the possibility of asking these people to help open doors into companies.

Funds can also be raised from employees through Give As You Earn, which allows staff to make regular, tax-efficient donations to their choice of charities through deductions from their pay.

A growing area of employee support is through volunteering. Although side-lined by some charities in favour of monetary support, employee volunteering can often be of equal, or greater, value to charities.

4 Transferring resources

Another source of return to charities from companies involves the transfer of resources (gifts in kind) or the temporary transfer of staff (secondment). A company may find it more cost effective to give its own products (or equipment that is no longer needed) than a cash donation: for example, IBM's community investment policy includes a programme of donating its products to charities.

Gifts in kind and secondments can not only be very valuable to charities in their own right but can also open the door to future, more profitable, partnerships. A number of charities are now using this approach as a point of entry into the corporate sector, an approach that has helped Children's Aid Direct become Number 5 in the corporate fundraising charity league (Corporate Citizen, 1998) with 58 per cent of its income now deriving from companies (see Chapter 13).

The management of corporate fundraising

Human resources

A good corporate fundraiser requires specialist skills: as a result, experienced staff are often in short supply. The fundraiser needs to be an individual who is credible at senior corporate level, commercially aware and an excellent communicator. This individual will need to be an ambassador for the cause as well as the internal champion of the benefits of corporate partnerships within their charity. An often-overlooked, but key, skill required is that of innovation and creativity.

Where a charity has a number of corporate fundraising staff, it was not uncommon for staff to be structured by *function*, with individual team members having responsibility for a *technique* such as employee fundraising or promotions. Now, however, a number of charities have adopted the account management structure used in advertising agencies, so that fundraisers are responsible for a number of companies or 'accounts'. With this wider brief, they aim to help their corporate partners meet their objectives for charitable support by developing tailor-made programmes.

Seeking out new business opportunities and making initial approaches to companies may be the responsibility of each corporate fundraiser or the specific remit of the head of corporate fundraising. Macmillan Cancer Relief, for example, is structured so that the new business is handled by 'hunters' based in the national office, and the day-to-day account management by locally based 'farmers'.

(For a more detailed account of the issues surrounding human resources, see Chapter 8.)

How corporate fundraising links with and affects other areas of fundraising

For a strategy of corporate fundraising to work, everyone from the trustees down has to be committed to the programme and to investing the time and resources needed to make a success of it.

Far from being an isolated team within a charity, the corporate fundraising department should work closely with other fundraising departments and be fully supported by the charity's functional departments.

The impact on all areas of operation for a charity undertaking a corporate fundraising programme can be considerable:

- The service provision side of the charity will need to communicate projects suitable for corporate support and be prepared to host visits for, or give presentations to, existing and potential corporate donors.
- The accounts department needs to be geared up to receive corporate donations and be fully conversant with the relevant tax laws.
- The company secretary may need to advise on the legal aspects of corporate fundraising; if the charity is going to be involved in sponsorship or promotions, the company secretary should advise on whether a trading company should be set up to avoid corporation tax.
- The PR department should work closely with the corporate fundraisers to generate PR for partnerships and to ensure the publications and messages being communicated are appropriate for the corporate market place.
- Ideally a charity-wide database will be needed to cross-reference donors and track all inter-relationships; this will require the input and support of the charity's IT expertise.
- All fundraising departments should liaise closely to ensure that donors have one main contact and are not bombarded with mass approaches from different fundraisers. In particular, the relationship between the national and regional corporate fundraising operations needs careful consideration. A networked database is a very useful way of noting key contacts.

Leonard Cheshire Foundation has instigated a system whereby companies are given a red, green or amber code. Regionally based staff can approach green companies of their own accord, amber companies only after discussion with the national operation, and red companies not at all, since these will be targeted on a national basis (for more information on this system, see p 78).

Ways to improve your corporate fundraising

A charity seeking to raise money from the corporate sector needs to be able to demonstrate why a company should support its cause rather than another. A clear understanding of a charity's unique selling propositions (USPs) is therefore vital, as is an investment in promotional materials, such as a corporate brochure and a credentials document for presentations to potential supporters.

Investing in research

Research is a vital means for the corporate fundraiser to keep informed of developments and key personalities in the corporate world, and of voluntary-sector news. For this reason, some charities have a researcher based in the corporate fundraising department.

Research can also be a valuable way of gaining a clear picture of a charity's supporters, its level of awareness and its reputation with the public – and it need not be costly: adding questions about a charity to an omnibus survey is an inexpensive exercise.

A clear idea of its existing and potential supporters, and of the importance the public attached to its cause, has helped Tommy's Campaign gain substantial support from the corporate sector: of its 1996–97 income of only £1.8 million, 47 per cent was raised from companies.

Using PR

Companies are more likely to support a well-known charity that they consider a safe bet, particularly in the case of cause-related marketing. Becoming better known in the business world can therefore give a charity the edge.

A charity can increase its profile by submitting press releases to targeted media about existing partnerships and successes, organising events (for example, receptions) specifically aimed at the corporate world, and using influential supporters to spread the word.

A more expensive option is to invest in advertising directly for potential corporate partners, a route that has been pursued by a number of charities. Advertising over a sustained period can be effective in generating awareness of the charity and keep a charity in the front of the minds of corporates seeking a partnership.

Many corporate partners will have a particular need for publicity, and it is therefore important that the corporate fundraiser can draw on the resources of the charity's communications specialists. Some charities have fulfilled this need by allocating a PR officer to major projects, or even having a dedicated corporate fundraising PR professional.

Networking and business groups

For every successful partnership a fundraiser builds, he or she will make many unsuccessful approaches. Developing opportunities to open up a dialogue with potential partners is a vital way of increasing the likelihood of success. As competition gets more and more fierce, the personal approach is the one that stands the greatest chance of success.

A number of charities have set up a 'development board' or 'industry committee' of 'the great and the good' to help them make friends and influence people in the corporate sector. Any charity, whatever its size, can use its contacts and pulling power to involve senior industry personnel, and can take full advantage of the concept of a development board.

A board can operate on a formal basis, with regular collective meetings, or may be a committee in name only: in this case, the fundraiser meets members individually and uses their expertise and contacts on an *ad-hoc* basis. Whichever approach is taken, the important thing is that the members of the board are committed to the charity and agree to help with contacts, advice and, possibly, ideas.

The success of a board depends on recruiting a good, and influential, chairman. The fact that Save The Children has had HRH The Princess Royal as the Chair of its Industry Committee has enabled it to make great in-roads to the corporate sector.

Who should sit on the board?

The seniority of those invited on board depends on the charity's needs and the accessibility of the contacts available to a charity, but members should clearly be decision makers and budget holders within their companies. It is important to target people of a common level of seniority so they feel they are being asked to join a peer group.

Most people are flattered to be asked to join a board and may welcome the opportunity to network informally with other business people. However, some 'names' are in great demand from charities: investing in research to identify up-and-coming entrepreneurs can pay dividends.

A development board needs regular maintenance to work to peak efficiency, since the charity is likely to be secondary to the main priorities of the board members. Specify what members are required to do and spoon feed them where necessary: for example, when asking members for contacts, a draft list on which they can indicate who they know can be very helpful.

Other networks available for a charity to exploit for corporate fundraising include the contacts of its trustees, its existing supporters and its suppliers.

Major donors

According to the Pareto Principle, in any marketing exercise 80 per cent of business comes from 20 per cent of a company's customers: this is also true of corporate fundraising.

Identifying a charity's key or 'major donors' enables it to concentrate on the areas where there is the greatest chance of long-term income. This applies to individual major donors as it does to corporate major donors. It is the reason why the corporate fundraiser must know if the director of a target company is an individual donor in his or her own right, so that the approach may be tailored accordingly and the individual not bombarded with appeals from different areas of the charity.

Where fundraisers managing corporate donors and those managing major donors work closely together to identify opportunities, there is greater potential to maximise fundraising and contacts. Individuals can play key roles across the fundraising divide: for example, the chairman of an industry committee who is the managing director of a corporate supporter can be also be developed as a major donor.

Measuring success

Evaluating corporate projects

A charity that monitors and evaluates each project it is involved in will be in a strong position to build on its successes and to use this information to increase support from existing and potential supporters. For example, producing a review document of a sponsorship activity detailing how objectives were met and what benefits were received by the company and the charity can help the former make a positive decision about future involvement. Presentation of this document will also give the charity an opportunity to schedule a meeting with the company.

Evaluating corporate fundraising strategy

Some charities use benchmarking to evaluate their fundraising strategy, including that of the corporate fundraising operation. 'Fundratios' are a benchmarking tool, developed by the Centre for Interfirm Comparison, that allows evaluation of a charity's performance against that of other charities in a number of areas, for example in terms of how much each fundraiser raises. However, such statistics come with a health warning: charities have different ways of calculating expenditure and income, so like is not always compared with like.

What is vital is that the means for monitoring and evaluating a project form part of the plan drawn up by the corporate fundraising department (which will also outline objectives and strategy) and that each team member takes responsibility for their part in achieving this plan.

Evaluation of CCI by companies

More and more companies are evaluating their support of charities against set objectives. A recent initiative by the London Benchmarking Group – a group consisting of six companies originally, now expanded to eighteen – sets out to evaluate and compare the overall effect of each member company's CCI programme against the others in the group.

Assessing profitability

Success in corporate fundraising does not happen overnight, and a charity may have to make a considerable investment for it to work. The charity's trustees must therefore understand and support the long-term nature of corporate fundraising (in turn determined by company budget lead times), and the need to invest resources and have professionally trained staff. It is unrealistic to expect an investment in corporate fundraising to start paying off before year 3.

After such an initial set-up period, many charities use an income/cost ratio to evaluate their fundraising activities: NSPCC, for example, uses a ratio of 4:1. It must however be appreciated that any *new* initiative, for example embarking on a corporate mailing programme, is unlikely to achieve such ratios in the early stages. This is not to say that such initiatives are not worth the investment – they are often valuable ways of developing new areas of activity or of innovation – merely that such investment should not be made on the assumption of an immediately high income/cost ratio.

Conclusion

A properly managed, well-resourced corporate fundraising department – with good account management, a successful new business strategy, and an eye for new opportunities – has the potential to bring rich rewards to a charity. Efforts spent on developing major corporate donors and building long-term relationships with companies are likely to be roundly repaid since, as competition increases, the most successful charities will be those that look after their corporate partners best.

CHAPTER FOUR

Investing in strategy

Brian Roberts-Wray

The need for a corporate fundraising strategy

The long-term imperative

If fundraising is all about building and sustaining relationships with supporters, it follows that corporate fundraising is concerned with the same process, but with business enterprises. Corporate fundraising is not separate from the rest of a charity's fundraising programme: the difference between effective fundraising from individual donors and fundraising from the corporate sector is not one of philosophy and approach, but of technique and style.

Any business with which a charity could have a productive dialogue about supporting its cause is going to be operating against long-term objectives and plans. Businesses are therefore more likely to support charities that operate in accordance with similar disciplines to their own, rather than with causes that appear to fly by the seat of their pants: each party to the dialogue has to feel comfortable with the culture of the other. The first imperative in corporate fundraising is therefore for a charity to take a long-term view and develop a clear strategic framework to accommodate its corporate fundraising plans, and not just because it is a good discipline in its own right.

Linking with the overall fundraising strategy

This chapter assumes that you have already defined a fundraising strategy, that it enjoys genuine support throughout your organisation, and that it includes a commitment to make a success of corporate fundraising. This last is important, because what we are considering here is really a sub-strategy, not a free-standing initiative in its own right. You are going to deploy the same basic philosophy and approach to corporate work as to the rest of your fundraising portfolio, so it is essential that your corporate fundraising strategy should be totally consistent with the strategic approach you are adopting overall. As with individual donors, businesses are going to support you only if they can identify with the values and beliefs to which your organisation adheres. If you appear to potential corporate donors to have a different agenda from the rest of the organisation, you will succeed only in sowing confusion and possibly suspicion. It is vital that corporate fundraisers sing from the same song-sheet as their direct marketing and community fundraising colleagues. If they do not, they will get nowhere.

Corporate fundraising without a clear strategy behind it is doomed to failure, and that corporate fundraising strategy must be consistent with – indeed, must be an integral part of – your overall fundraising strategy. The rest of this chapter will focus on the essential elements of a corporate fundraising strategy, and the disciplines you need to adopt to develop one.

Setting strategic objectives

Basic principles

Setting clear objectives is always the starting point for developing a strategy: these objectives have to be time-specific, but how far ahead you plan depends on a number of factors, including the size and maturity of your organisation, planning procedures in other disciplines and the rate of change envisaged in the service-provision environment in which you operate. As a general rule, a five-year strategy is a sensible timescale: there will be occasions when anything beyond three years becomes academic; conversely, although more rarely, even a ten-year plan can be valid.

Financial objectives

Financial objectives are obviously the most important set of objectives to define and those in which your trustees or management board are going to be most interested. The vital thing is to keep them simple and to paint with a broad brush. The objectives should therefore:

- focus on Year 5 (assuming a five-year planning cycle) and avoid the temptation of setting annual staging posts – at the most you could indicate one mid-point objective;
- be expressed in terms of net contribution (ie gross income less direct costs): it is valid to indicate how that net contribution will be achieved, by quoting both gross income and cost targets, but you should make it clear that it is the net contribution figure that represents the formal objective – a target for the cost–income ratio should be included as a subsidiary objective to ensure the operation is being run cost-effectively;

- be quoted in round figures – long-term planning is never an exact science, and to present a five-year forecast that claims accuracy closer than the nearest £10,000 is an exercise in futility.

Operational objectives

In addition to the financial objectives, you may wish to establish operational objectives, such as how many companies will have concluded long-term supportive arrangements with you by the end of the period, or how many pieces of new business will have been generated. Again, keep them simple and, above all, make sure they are measurable. There is no point in setting an objective against which performance cannot be objectively assessed.

Qualitative objectives

Part of your reason for espousing corporate fundraising may be that you wish to raise awareness of your charity and its service provision, either among the business community itself, or by using business as a conduit to reaching the public. If this is the case, it is valid to include a formal objective to reflect this aspiration, although you should also recognise that, even with the use of mechanisms like research, it may be difficult to attribute results directly to the corporate initiative.

Review of options

Rationale

A strategy is rather like a map. Once you have identified the objectives, you know where it is on the map that you wish to go. The next decision to make is which route to take to get there: this involves reviewing all options in a number of areas that will be outlined in the following paragraphs.

Structure and resourcing

How will corporate fundraising fit into the structure of the department? Some will argue for it to be a part of field fundraising; others will prefer it to be free standing and independent of other parts of the department. In the latter case, how the interface between corporate fundraising and field fundraising is managed will need to be addressed. How corporate fundraisers will relate to other members of the department is of critical importance, as are the number and seniority of corporate fundraisers, and their experience mix. All these factors must be critically and objectively examined as part of the strategy-setting exercise.

Geographical options

You need to consider carefully whether your corporate fundraising effort is going to be national, whether you are going to test market in one region before extending to national coverage, or whether you are going to focus on areas where your charity is well known or has some physical asset. The natural tendency is often to approach larger national companies, but analysis of your charity's geographical and other strengths may lead to more effective targeting.

Corporate focus – industrial sector

Deciding which industrial sector you are going to concentrate your efforts on is both a negative and a positive process. First, you have to decide whether there are any 'no-go areas', such as tobacco companies, armaments, chemicals, nuclear power, etc (see Chapter 7). Then you have to select industrial sectors for priority treatment, which will normally depend on where the activities of your organisation best achieve a 'fit' with an industrial sector. It may seem obvious for medical charities to seek links with the pharmaceutical industry, for animal welfare charities to go for veterinary suppliers and for charities providing mobility for disabled people to target the transportation industry, but it is important to review all the possibilities – often a little lateral thinking can yield a surprising, but highly persuasive, piece of targeting.

Corporate focus – point of entry

It is important to review where you are going in order to position your corporate approaches. A strategy targeting community-affairs budgets is likely to differ from one seeking cause-related marketing partnerships. Chapters 2 and 3 of this book elaborate the options available to fundraisers making approaches to companies.

Charity focus

It is important to review all the options in terms of specific projects or aspects of your service delivery – you could use this as a hook on which to hang an appeal for corporate support. No business is going to support your charity just because of its name and reputation: they will want to know precisely how their support is going to make a difference. The more specific the case, the more likely it is to succeed. Some charities, for whom general unrestricted donations are a priority, often see this is as a stumbling block, but the 'packaging' of areas of work into a shopping list can be extremely effective.

Setting priorities

Applying qualitative criteria

The purpose of reviewing all the options available to you, as outlined above, is that it enforces a disciplined approach to strategy setting. The same disciplined approach must be used in making an objective decision about which options you are going to set aside and which you will put resources into. Some thought needs to be given to the criteria you are going to apply in selecting, for example, no more than five out of ten possible options. Once you have decided on the criteria, stick with them – even if it produces a priority which is against your 'gut feel'!

Timing

Having identified a short list of initiatives you want to go with, you have to recognise that it is impossible to do them all at the same time, without making a hash of it. More hard decisions have to be made in determining what you are going to do this year and what may have to wait three or four years before it may be tackled.

Resourcing the programme

Internal resource

Having reviewed your options in structure and resourcing for your corporate fundraising programme, you now have to decide how you are going to implement the selected option. How many people will you need to recruit, and will they come from internal or external sources? Which posts are you going to fill first, and what will the recruitment and employment costs be? Where are the new team members going to sit, and what will they need in terms of secretarial assistance, IT facilities, etc? These are the issues that must be addressed at this stage.

External resource

You need to decide whether the programme can be entirely internally driven or whether you need to bring in some external resource to support you. Will you need a marketing agency or some other specialist consultant assistance in order to achieve your objectives? What you decide will depend on the type of programme you adopt, but you need to plan strategically for an outside resource if you need it, otherwise you will wake up one morning and discover that you do not have the tools to do the next week's work.

Time phasing

By this stage of the strategy-setting process, you will have identified several major initiatives or projects that need to be implemented. The phasing of these major activities should be built into the strategy: in many cases there will be significant capital or revenue costs involved in advance of the project launch that need to be planned for.

Budgeting within the strategy

Five-year plan and annual budget

Some people think that the existence of a five-year plan makes annual budgeting superfluous. It does not. A strategic plan is not five annual plans piled on top of each other. To return to the analogy of the map, if a strategic plan is a map showing the start point, the objective and the route to be taken over a period of several years, an annual budget is a larger-scale map of part of the route that takes into account short-term variations, like road works. In short, the strategic plan is a broad framework of action, whereas the annual budget is a detailed plan for a limited time period, aiming at the same objective, but guided and informed by short-term phenomena that were not in evidence at the time the strategy was devised. Normally, the existence of a strategic plan will make the annual budget exercise more straightforward.

Fundamentals of budget planning

A corporate fundraising budget comprises two elements: an activity schedule and an estimate of the income and cost implications of putting that activity schedule into action. There is a tendency to regard budgeting merely as a number-crunching exercise, but it has value as a management tool only if the activity schedule forms an integral part of it. The annual budget has strategic relevance only if it takes the strategic plan as its starting point and reacts to it. In some organisations, once the strategic plan has been agreed, it gathers dust on the shelf and is never referred to again; in other organisations, the strategic plan is treated as Holy Writ and slavishly followed regardless of short-term environmental, competitive or regulatory pressures. These extremes are equally wrong: a strategic plan should remain your guidebook, but the annual budget gives you frequent opportunities to review not the objectives, but the precise means of achieving them in the light of experience.

Building in flexibility

One of the difficulties with corporate fundraising is that it usually comprises a small number of large transactions, which means that the failure of one planned activity to materialise or to deliver in the way planned can have a disproportional effect on the whole annual performance. This problem also has an opportunity built into it. This chapter has concentrated on the importance of long-term planning, but, where a charity has a good reputation in working with businesses, opportunities will from time to time materialise out of the blue. It is essential to be able to react resourcefully to such opportunities, but the problem is that they cannot be budgeted for. You can however build in an opportunity contingency budget, which takes account of the fact that the unexpected always happens at least once a year! Alternatively, peaks and troughs in income can be managed by the use of a rolling three-year financial target.

Summary

- As with the rest of your fundraising programme, corporate fundraising is about building relationships, and the surest way to build effective relationships with businesses is to demonstrate that you work to similar disciplines to their own. That implies a commitment to long-term strategic planning.

- Your corporate fundraising strategy must be an integral part of your overall fundraising strategy. It also requires support from every part of your organisation, because the implementation of the strategy implies interdepartmental co-operation.

- The first stage of strategic planning for corporate fundraising involves setting long-term objectives, which will certainly include financial targets, but can also encompass operational and qualitative objectives.

- Once the objectives are set, it is necessary to review, objectively and without prejudice, all the possible ways of achieving them. This should result in firmly based programmes of fundraising activities, which will then need to be assigned priorities.

- Once the strategic programme is developed, it is necessary to plan how it is going to be resourced, both in terms of internal resource and also the support needed from external sources.

- The existence of a strategic plan that may cover five years does not render a detailed annual budgeting process superfluous, but it does make it easier, because it ensures that annual budgets are focused on long-term objectives. The annual budget also needs to contain an opportunity contingency element, to ensure that you always have sufficient flexibility to react to the unexpected.

Corporate fundraising strategy – format and layout

The following is not intended as a blueprint to be followed in all cases. It might, however, form a useful starting point for putting a corporate fundraising strategy down on paper, assuming that the disciplines advocated in this chapter have been followed.

BACKGROUND AND RESEARCH

- A short history of corporate fundraising in the organisation over the past five years
- A reference to the organisation's overall fundraising strategy, indicating how corporate fundraising fits into this

STRATEGIC OBJECTIVES

- *Financial*   Target net contribution from corporate fundraising for year 1, year 3 and year 5.
  How target is to be achieved in terms of gross income, direct costs and net contribution.
- *Operational* eg To achieve x Charity of the Year collaborations, y cause-related marketing initiatives and z logo-licensing agreements (including timescale within which these targets are seen).
- *Qualitative*   eg To enhance our reputation with major companies that have their own occupational health departments, to the point where our services are considered relevant to their occupational health programmes.

REGIONAL STRATEGY

Review possible options, as between a national approach, an exclusive focus on London, a particular regional bias, a single region pilot test, followed by a national roll-out, etc. End by defining priorities.

INDUSTRIAL SECTOR STRATEGY

Review options with all major industrial sectors, eg engineering, manufacturing, financial services, sport, tourism, retailing, etc. Define no-go areas and priority areas.

TYPE OF PARTNERSHIP

Review options as between seeking cash support, employee fundraising, cause-related marketing, gifts in kind, personnel secondments, etc. Define priorities.

Fundraising focus

Review options on which part of your charity's operations you want corporate fundraising to support, eg core funding, development projects, building work, special events sponsorship, etc. Define priorities.

Resourcing the strategy

Internal resource
Outline recruitment and training needs to deliver the strategy. Consider the implications for office accommodation, IT systems, etc. Include implications on other departments in the organisation, which might need to gear up their resource to service the corporate fundraising strategy, in particular PR resource.

External resource
Review the possible need for contracting the services of marketing agencies, consultants, etc in order to implement the strategy.

Time plan
Indicate critical timings on major parts of the strategic plan.

Research
Indicate any areas where research (desk research, qualitative or quantitative market research) will be needed in order to validate or inform aspects of the strategic plan. Indicate timing and likely costs of such research.

Five-year financial model

Make clear that the tabulated figures supplied here are not a year-by-year forecast of financial out-turn (these forecasts will appear as part of each year's budget-setting routine) but an indication of likely movements in income and expenditure that would result from successful implementation of the corporate fundraising strategic plan.

Also indicate which costs should be regarded as investment costs, as distinct from annually recurring costs.

Add an 'opportunity contingency' element to each year's projected figures.

Appendices

Be prepared to include appendices where supplementary information might be useful to the reader of the document, even if not essential. Appendices could cover, for example, subjects like a SWOT analysis, a case history, a list of priority or 'no-go' companies, etc.

CHAPTER FIVE

Making corporate fundraising work

Andrew Craven

Beyond the feel-good factor

The unique thing about corporate fundraising is that it offers you the opportunity of working in the voluntary sector while maintaining strong links with the private sector – its motivations, its resources and its successes. In addition to having a foot in both sectors, corporate fundraising also offers practitioners the opportunity of working within a field that requires a range of disciplines, which can include: marketing, public relations, sponsorship, advertising and communications. Collectively, this represents a very challenging environment in which to work; if done correctly, it can play one of the most significant parts in any organisation's overall fundraising strategy.

One of the first things to learn about working with companies is that they often work at a different timescale from those within your organisation. If you are hoping to secure significant support in the form of sponsorship or a cause-related marketing project, you must appreciate that a company sets its budgets well in advance of its new financial year: going to a company for support you require in the next few months is unlikely to succeed; going to a company for support you will need in 18 months' time stands a much better chance.

To secure the highest returns, an effective corporate fundraising strategy needs to appreciate, and to be able to direct, the resources it has at its disposal. A strategy that focuses limited resources on only a handful of corporate supporters is likely to result in a higher level of support than a strategy that requires the same resources to reach all the FTSE 100 companies.

What's in it for companies?

Wherever an organisation decides to direct its corporate fundraising resources, it will inevitably ask the question 'What is in it for us?' The task of a corporate fundraiser is to succeed in cracking this question with each of the companies it approaches.

The straightforward 'feel-good factor' has all but disappeared from the list of possible answers, certainly for larger levels of support. Corporate fundraisers need to understand the motivations and various business needs companies have, and how the project or work for which support is sought might tap into these. This often requires a corporate fundraiser to look at the work of their organisation from a different perspective from that which a legacy fundraiser or those working in direct marketing might. For example, a corporate fundraiser needs to understand that a company may not only be interested in how many donors a charity has: who its donors are (do they match the customers they are trying to reach?) and where the charity works (does its geographical location match areas of company presence or areas they would like to break into?) may be as important as the work itself.

While 'making the match' is very important, it does not always have to be sophisticated. Companies may simply be interested in some local publicity in an area where they have offices/factories, or they may be interested in encouraging their employees to support their local community, via volunteering. At the other end of the scale, companies may wish to enter into a cause-related campaign in order to give them a clear advantage over their competitors.

Whatever the answer, companies will expect you to deliver, and a golden rule to remember is never to promise more than can be confidently delivered. Some relationships may place few demands on an organisation while others, especially large-scale sponsorships, may require an organisation to deliver across a whole range of activities. These can consume internal resources; if these are not in place, the relationship will not succeed. It is easy to offer the world when a significant donation is in your reach, but saying you will do something and then not delivering will have serious consequences for the future. Be realistic. Do not, for example, guarantee press coverage when everyone (including the company) knows that such things cannot be guaranteed.

Methods of winning new business

There are many ways in which an organisation can secure new corporate donors. Resources should always be channelled in such a way as to maximise returns. A successful corporate fundraising programme will incorporate a range of methods to secure new support. Where budgets are limited, different methods will have to be considered and chosen between, and the final choice will depend upon budgets available, and the ability to cope with potential responses.

Listed below are some of the options to be considered.

The 'numbers game' – direct marketing and telemarketing

To use these approaches, it is important to understand the disciplines of such marketing, and the resource implications. Direct marketing and telemarketing can reach a vast corporate audience – ideal in emergency situations such as raising money for disaster relief – but are more likely to result in low-level support. Some charities have used direct marketing and telemarketing successfully to generate initial appointments. But it is interesting to ponder over the reaction of corporate personnel who are on the receiving ends of these methods. To harness the real capacity within the corporate sector the approach has to be personalised to an extent that is not usually possible in these disciplines.

Personalised approaches

An alternative option, whatever means of corporate fundraising you are undertaking (whether it be employee appeals, corporate sponsorship or cause-related marketing), is to target specific companies with a personalised proposal.

Showing that you have taken the time to get to know the company and have realistically matched your work to their possible needs (it is always going to be difficult to know exactly what a company's needs will be, but you should be able to gain a fair idea) indicates a more serious intention than a general letter drop.

Peer recommendation

As with all other areas of marketing, one of the most successful methods of generating new business is through personal recommendation. Whether that is through the setting up of a Development Board to 'spread the word' on your behalf, as discussed in Chapter 3, or through effectively managing and capitalising on successful existing partnerships, this is a method appropriate to all charities.

Proposals and presentations

How do you make your proposal stand out from the rest? Despite what some people might think, the smarter-looking proposal is not necessarily the winner. Companies are driven by clear business needs, and it is the substance of the proposal that counts to them, not the aesthetics (though these can help).

Research

To make a bespoke proposal you must first get to know the company. Research therefore plays an important part in the overall process, perhaps the most important part. Among the things you will need to find out are the following:

- who the company is (not as straightforward as it sounds – Shell plc alone has numerous subsidiary companies, all of which have Shell in their title);
- what it does;
- where it is located;
- what its current business strategies are and what their existing charitable/community policy is (if they have one);
- what number of employees it has, and what its internal operating structures are;
- who its major competitors are.

Only when you have some or all of this information can you begin to establish whether or not the company is a match for your project and to answer the question of what is in it for them, if they support you.

There is no excuse for not doing this research. There is a wealth of information currently available to corporate fundraisers, ranging from reference books such as Hemmington Scott's *The Corporate Register* and Dunn and Bradstreet's *Key British Enterprises* to state-of-the-art on-line systems such as *FT Profile* and *FT Discovery* (both to be found on www.ftep.ft.com) – all of which should be available from any major library if you do not have the budget to purchase them yourself. Alternatively, use the telephone! While not usually the right medium to make a request for support, phoning a company is an ideal way to gather information and to confirm details that you may already have found out. Many companies, especially the larger ones, have Corporate Affairs Departments (or something similar) which will be pleased to send you their latest annual report or more detailed information on their products and community affairs policy. At worst, a receptionist or telephonist will be able to help clarify basic details such as names and titles.

Corporate fundraising is also one area of fundraising where your trustees, colleagues and suppliers (especially your legal advisers and accountants) can be very helpful to you. Their knowledge of a company you wish to approach can often complement what you have already put together from more· conventional sources. They may also be important players in the process of making an approach.

Written proposals

The findings of your research may have utterly convinced you that the company you are targeting is the perfect match – *they* will need to be convinced. It is therefore worth spending a little time looking at how you put your case on paper.

Initial proposals should be short, easy to understand and personalised. A general proposal that could as easily be given to any other company will be seen as just that. These initial proposals, and even later ones, do not have to be sophisticated in terms of the quality of materials or the level of design used. The most important thing is the proposition, which must be simple and easy to understand.

Present an outline that summarises the project and clarifies how the company could benefit from becoming involved. Make it clear that you would welcome its input, or that of any agencies it uses, to take full advantage of the opportunities available. Do not use jargon and do not lapse into terminology that is internal to your organisation. Where appropriate, use language that relates to the company's business activity (on the understanding that you know what it means). When listing benefits, be clear about exactly what you are offering: for example, it is common to acknowledge support in an organisation's annual report, but highlighting how many reports are produced and who they go to will make this more attractive. The same principle applies to such things as promotional leaflets: how many will you produce, who will they be distributed to, and where?

Do not be afraid to include within the proposal a very brief summary of the other companies you have worked with successfully. This gives you credibility: companies, just like individuals, like to be associated with success.

The proposal should be accompanied by appropriate materials and a short covering letter that highlights the key points of the proposal. However, no matter how good your proposal is, do not expect the company to call you back. To ascertain the company's interest you should be prepared to follow the proposal up with a call (closing a covering letter with 'I will call you in a few days to discuss this opportunity further' makes the call much easier to make) and offer to meet the company's representatives, face to face.

Whether you should submit a written proposal before the meeting, or only after it, will be for you to decide. Some corporate fundraisers prefer to call first and take the initial written proposal with them to the meeting; others prefer to send a brief proposal first. Whichever route you take, a meeting early on in the proceedings is essential.

Meetings and presentations

There are training course dedicated to 'effective meetings' – rightly so, because knowing how to perform well in them can make all the difference.

Establishing a rapport with the donor is as important in corporate fundraising as it is in other areas of fundraising such as major gifts and legacies. As well as researching the company, you should therefore research who you are going to meet. In addition to establishing the relationship, meetings offer the opportunity for you to clarify what you have already mentioned in the proposal and to learn from the company representatives what aspects caught their imagination – as this was not a definitive document you can, within reason, incorporate their ideas, which gives them ownership of the project. Be prepared to respond to the unseen, and be flexible. Very often the final relationship will be a departure from your original idea but, as long as you still get what you require, that should not be a problem.

A point worth noting is that your network of contacts could be invaluable in identifying a link with the company – as such, they may be the person to make the initial contact. So long as they understand what is being asked of the company, you should not be afraid of allowing your best contact to put their name to a proposal and attend, if willing, the first meeting – a warm approach is always better than a cold one, so a known contact could make all the difference.

Managing the relationship

There are perhaps two tests to the success of a corporate fundraising team: one is the internal achievement of targets; the second is the professional delivery of what has been promised. A corporate supporter is rarely interested in the former but will be extremely preoccupied with the latter.

What it takes to maintain a good working relationship with a corporate supporter, especially larger donors, should not be underestimated. As far as the company is concerned, you have entered into an agreement, and the company will expect you to honour your side of the bargain – a further reason why you should not offer more than you can deliver.

One of the easiest ways to maintain a good working relationship with a corporate supporter is to regard them as a client and treat them as an advertising agency would treat its clients. What they need is 'client handling', which often means that they will expect to deal with just one or two individuals at all times, they will require regular updates on progress, and they will expect to be consulted at all stages (especially where the use of their logo is concerned – this alone can be time consuming). Evaluation reports are also becoming a key feature of corporate fundraising: companies want to know what their investment in your work has achieved, not only for you, but for them too. This can be crucial in respect to a company's potential for future support. What form the evaluation report takes will depend on what the company requires of you, so it is important to clarify this early in the relationship.

Again, like many aspects of fundraising, you stand more chance of securing further support from your current donors than you do of securing support from new prospects. You should therefore view the delivery of the relationship as a long-term investment, and to strengthen it you should be prepared to learn continuously about the company and about the key people within it. Getting to know different people at different levels within the company helps to cement the relationship. This can be important at a time when the company is deliberating whether to continue its support, or when your contact leaves the company.

The contract

A contract or letter of agreement can make the delivery of the relationship easier. Clearly outlining the role of each party at the outset will act as an indication of what should be delivered, by when, and by whom. Like many aspects of corporate fundraising, it is worth spending some time in drafting a contract or letter of agreement, as it could save a great deal of time in the future when issues are contested. Even with a small relationship with a small local company it is worth preparing some formal agreement. Large corporate sponsorships may require contracts that only legal advisers can prepare (in which case, you need to be aware of the cost implications and if possible build this into the support you are seeking from the donor).

Any letter or contract should, as a minimum, cover several key points: clarification of the project and the parties involved; details of what each party has agreed to bring to the project and by when; explanation of benefits offered; clarification of financial arrangements (for example, payment might be staggered over a period of months or required in one lump sum).

A point worth noting is that contracts or letters of agreement should also be prepared for gifts in kind (in the form of either equipment or services). You need to ensure that the in-kind-support you are receiving is of the exact specification you require and will be delivered within a time frame that does not jeopardise the completion of the project.

Building your portfolio

Success breeds success. Being able to highlight a proven track record gives your proposal or presentation a credibility others might lack. Keep examples from other projects of materials you produced, copies of media coverage you secured and, better still, any feedback you have received from previous corporate donors. An endorsement from them could count for a great deal.

By working with a range of companies you will also inevitably build up a portfolio of errors, things that did not go to plan. Omitting sponsors' credits on key materials, missing deadlines, not actually delivering what you promised or simply being scuppered by another arm of your organisation are just some of the mistakes you will learn from!

CHAPTER SIX

Cause-related marketing – who benefits and how?

Sue Adkins

Introduction and background

The simple answer to the question posed in the chapter title is that, if cause-related marketing is done well, everyone benefits: the charity or cause, the business, the consumer and, indeed, if leveraged particularly effectively, the supply and distribution chain too.

The phrase 'cause-related marketing' was apparently coined by American Express in the 1980s. American Express had been invited to become a commercial sponsor for the restoration of the Statue of Liberty. Rather than take up this opportunity, American Express decided instead to run a sales promotion based on the theme of the restoration of the Statue of Liberty. Building on the success of previous promotions linked to charities, American Express ran a cause-related marketing promotion between September and December 1983.

The mechanic was straightforward. Existing customers were invited to use their American Express card, and new customers were invited to apply for an American Express Card. Every time the card was used, a donation was made to the Restoration of the Statue of Liberty Fund. For each new card application, a larger sum was donated.

By the end of the three-month promotion, over $1.7 million had been raised for the cause; American Express was reported to have seen a 28 per cent increase in card use in the first month and a 45 per cent increase in new card applications. Since then, American Express has run over 90 cause-related marketing programmes in 17 different countries (see Adkins, 1999, for a more detailed account of this case study).

Defining cause-related marketing

There was no agreed definition of what cause-related marketing was until the Business in the Community Cause Related Marketing Campaign was set up to develop cause-related marketing as a formal and well-resourced part of the marketing mix. The overall goal of the initiative was to generate awareness and understanding of cause-related marketing and to encourage business to use the marketing of their products and services to benefit their business and charities or causes and the wider community.

As part of this mission it was important to come to an agreed definition of cause-related marketing. The definition that Business in the Community (BitC) emerged with – which the industry has generally accepted as appropriate – is a commercial activity by which businesses and charities or causes form a partnership with each other to market an image, product or service for mutual benefit. It is nothing more than enlightened self-interest: cause-related marketing is not about altruism or philanthropy.

The key words in this definition are 'commercial', 'partnership' and 'mutual benefit'. Cause-related marketing is a partnership between the cause or charity and the business: neither side has greater weight, value or importance in the equation; integrity, transparency, sincerity, mutual respect, partnership and mutual benefit are the key principles underpinning cause-related marketing, as set out in the BitC Cause Related Marketing Guidelines. (These guidelines, the first such in the world, were developed in consultation with business, charities, consumers and representative bodies and published in July 1997; they are available from BitC.)

Cause-related marketing is a strategic tool

The more strategic the application of cause-related marketing is, the better. Implemented as part of an overall Corporate Community Investment (CCI) programme, it can provide many benefits to a whole range of stakeholder groups, including employees, customers and charities, as well as the wider community, suppliers, and opinion formers. It can enhance corporate and brand reputation through strategic long-term relationships between businesses and charities or causes that seek to enhance corporate values while at the same time contributing to the mission of the cause.

Cause-related marketing involves any activity where the link with a cause or charity has been developed in order to support the marketing of the business, while also contributing to the mission of the cause. In this account of cause-related marketing, it is clear that marketing is the operative word.

Cause-related marketing can address many objectives. From the perspective of the charity or cause, this can include all manner of resource: product, premises, profile, people, volunteers, new members, power, leverage from the business to attract other corporate partners, communication of new or existing messages or, indeed, straightforward cash. From the corporate point of view, objectives may range from enhancing corporate or brand reputation and values to building customer relationships and loyalty. It can also be effective in trialling new products, adding value, perhaps deflecting negative publicity and, indeed, building sales. This list of potential objectives is not exhaustive: the potential menu of objectives is vast. In many respects, the range of objectives that cause-related marketing can deliver is largely interchangeable between a charity, cause and business.

Evidence of the effect of cause-related marketing

Research carried out by Research International (UK) Ltd makes clear the potential strengths and benefits of cause-related marketing. Three key studies provide the picture from the business and the consumer perspective: *The Winning Game*, a major quantitative consumer survey of 1,053 individuals, *The Corporate Survey II*, conducted among 450 major UK companies, and *The Game Plan*, which included over 100 in-store consumer interviews and six focus groups around the country. Together, these pieces of research provide key evidence of the likely influence cause-related marketing could have on consumer buying habits and their perceptions of companies. This research also identifies the level of company involvement and, together, these pieces of research provide some of the essential background information to enable both charities and business to develop their case. These studies found the following:

- 86 per cent of consumers agree that, when price and quality are equal, they are more likely to buy a product associated with a 'cause';
- 73 per cent of consumers agree they would switch from one brand to another, price and quality being equal;
- 61 per cent agreed that they would change retail outlet for the same reason;
- 86 per cent of consumers agree that they have a more positive image of a company if they see it is doing something to make the world a better place;
- 64 per cent of consumers feel that cause-related marketing should be a standard part of a company's business practice;
- 70 per cent of marketing directors, 75 per cent of community affairs directors and 59 per cent of chief executives all believe that cause-related marketing will increase in importance over the next 2–3 years.

(Business in the Community/Research International (UK) Ltd, 1996 and 1998)

The evidence of consumer support for cause-related marketing has been further supported by *The Game Plan*, a third study by Research International (UK) Ltd for BitC. *The Game Plan* qualitative research clearly shows consumer endorsement of cause-related marketing when it is planned, implemented and communicated effectively. Indeed, cause-related marketing provides an effective way of engaging the consumer not only rationally but also emotionally with the company or its brand. *The Game Plan* lists the following as some of the key points to emerge:

- consumers continue to view Cause Related Marketing as a positive approach that offers another means by which business and consumers can support charities or causes;
- consumers appreciate that Cause Related Marketing provides an easy way to support charities and causes in the course of their busy lives;
- consumer response to Cause Related Marketing programmes that they are aware of is enthusiastic;
- consumers familiar with Cause Related Marketing programmes agree that it can enhance corporate image and, if handled well, can increase customer loyalty and sales;
- practically, consumers are more likely to alter their buying behaviour if, in doing so, the results of their efforts are identified, communicated and celebrated – if the reward for their efforts is acknowledged, quantified and communicated, such that the individual feels a connection, this can be even better.

(Business in the Community/Research International (UK) Ltd, 1997)

The process

Before embarking on the quest to find appropriate partners, the organisation – charitable, cause or business – must be clear about its objectives, values and assets. This sounds obvious but, with the excitement and enthusiasm of a creative opportunity, these fundamental points can be overlooked. In more than a few cases, partners have not always fully considered the extent of what might be achieved through the potential cause-related marketing relationship. The full scope of the potential can be undervalued if the strategy and programme are not fully linked back into the organisation's mission. By the same token, with the enthusiasm for the initial idea, without a clear methodical process, unexpected costs and risks can emerge.

As with any partnership, clarity from the outset provides for a smoother process, more effective implementation and a foundation for clear assessment. Setting clear objectives and agreeing what the factors and criteria for success are also helps avoid any misunderstandings and enables the development of a well-planned and clearly communicated activity. Planning of this kind also serves to manage expectations while providing a framework for monitoring and evaluation.

Establishing clear aims and objectives

It is essential that both sides of the partnership focus on the key primary aims and that these are discussed openly. Having established this, it enables the factors critical to success to be identified and the appropriate monitoring and evaluation processes to be developed to reflect them. After all, failure to define success makes it difficult to assess whether success has been achieved! Investment of time and thought at the beginning of the process is therefore invaluable, as it serves to define, monitor and manage expectations.

When setting the primary objectives, it is important that both partners identify each other's requirements and, in so doing, are equally clear about the objectives, mission and values of their own organisation. This is as true of a charity as it is of a business. These objectives should be communicated openly to each partner.

In defining the objectives of a programme or relationship, it must be clear what is negotiable and what is not. Concern has been expressed in some quarters that cause-related marketing encourages charities to lose sight of their mission, to 'sell their souls'. The mission and values of the charity are at the heart of their foundation and should always be pre-eminent when considering and negotiating any partnership. The same is also true for a company or a brand. Failure to hold true to these values and mission is more a comment on the negotiators' skills than on cause-related marketing as a discipline.

Valuing your assets

When entering negotiations, it is vital to be clear about your organisation's assets: to know your value, to know your worth, to define what is negotiable and what is not. All these aspects should be considered as part of a cause-related marketing programme or, indeed, any partnership strategy. Valuing your assets is a key part of the initial process: in order to negotiate effectively, you need to be clear about what assets you already have and how valuable these might be to the partner. At the same time, you must also consider what the potential partner's assets are and how valuable they might be to your cause or mission. Not enough time can be spent clarifying the value of assets. There is, for example, no compulsion on charities, or indeed businesses, to include any particular asset in the negotiation. Cause-related marketing is a negotiated partnership that involves mutual benefit: mutual benefit is the ultimate objective. Both sides must be clear what is, and is not, available for negotiation, what the value of any particular asset is, and how, when, why and where it can be used. For effective cause-related marketing it is essential that both sides are clear and that neither is being, or feels, exploited. Should those beginning the quest for a partner or entering negotiations be unclear about their objectives or their negotiable assets, and should the value of what is sought or desired be unclearly defined, there can be dangers for either side. Cause-related marketing is as effective or as ineffective as the user.

Finding a partner

Even after identifying the objectives of the potential partnership and valuing your assets from the point of view of what is available for negotiation, finding the appropriate partner can be a time-consuming process.

Different organisations approach the search for partners in different ways: some respond to a speculative enquiry from an agency 'on behalf of a client'; others actively search for partners by understanding the profile and lifestyle of their donor or support base and matching this against prospective brands and corporate customer profiles. Whatever the route in, time spent clarifying the values and value of your organisation, providing a clear set of objectives, and taking care to understand the motivation of the potential partner is time well invested.

Methods of finding a partner

BitC/Research International (UK) (1998) identified the following trends in businesses' procedures for finding partners:

- 32 per cent of businesses use previous experience;
- 26 per cent have a formal policy;
- 23 per cent use existing contacts;
- 20 per cent use desk research;
- 18 per cent use recommendations;
- 10 per cent use stakeholder research.

Having identified a partner with appropriate values, target market and assets, and having started negotiations, creativity and leverage are key aspects of the discussion. It is essential that each aspect of the partnership works hard for your investment, within the framework of your values.

Cause-related marketing examples

There are examples of effective cause-related marketing in all industry sectors and causes. The two case studies that follow illustrate cause-related marketing programmes between major blue-chip organisations and causes. Cause-related marketing, however, is not the prerogative of such large organisations and causes. Size does not matter – it is the quality of thought and application that makes the difference: the partnership of Nambarrie, the 35-person tea company in Northern Ireland, with Action Cancer illustrates what a significant difference a well-thought-through and fully leveraged programme can achieve (this study is covered in greater detail in Adkins, 1999); Ben & Jerry's demonstrated their relationship with War Child through the sale of Peace Pops; the Tusk Trust developed a successful relationship with Debenhams, Top Shop and the *Young Telegraph*. In each case, both parties raised their profile, and funds were generated for the cause.

TWO EXAMPLES OF CAUSE-RELATED MARKETING

The strategic relationship between Cadbury Ltd and Save the Children demonstrated itself through the annual Cadbury Strollerthon event and sponsorship of the regional pantomime season. The Cadbury Strollerthon raised approximately £400,00 each year for One Small Step and Save the Children, as well as significantly raising awareness. From the point of view of Cadbury Ltd, the core values of the company were reinforced among their target market, and the event provided useful opportunities for product sampling.

Tesco Computers for Schools programme, based on a straightforward collector mechanic and now in its eighth year, has made a massive impact on IT resources in schools: it has provided over £50 million worth of computers and peripheral equipment to schools to date, which equates to more than one computer for every school in England, Scotland and Wales. Not only does the programme effectively communicate through TV, press and radio advertising, but it serves to bring communities together in active support of local schools. At the same time, this strategic cause-related marketing programme is leveraged through the business in terms of employee and store support. The programme has developed over time as a result of monitoring and evaluation: increased support is now provided through the breadth of equipment available, school helplines and teacher support. Since 1998, the programme has been linked with other brands such as Coca Cola, it has been extended to include petrol sales and the offer of IT support seminars to accompany the provision of computers (see Adkins, 1999, for a more detailed account of these two case studies).

Issues to consider

The potential rewards of cause-related marketing are enormous, but so are the risks. These risks include not only the financial and logistical risks but also, more fundamentally, the integrity, reputation and values that the charity, cause, corporate or brand has developed over decades (and, in some cases, centuries), and also the vital support of the various constituencies and stakeholders. Partners must be clear not only about what there is to gain but also about what there is at stake. A risk analysis is therefore essential for both sides. These concerns are well illustrated by the case study of a US arthritic pain relief product that linked with a US arthritis charity.

A MARRIAGE MADE IN HEAVEN?

The consumer proposition was essentially that, on purchase of the product (which was heavily branded with the charity's name), the purchaser would receive a discount. The money discounted would be donated to the charity, and the consumer would receive free membership of the charity for a year. Retailers selling the brand were involved in a range of activities promoting the product, so the programme was also leveraged through the distribution chain.

This was a programme from which everyone seemed to benefit. The gains to the charity appeared to be the high-profile awareness of the cause and the presence of the product: the advertising and other forms of communication provided significant awareness and apparently generated a financial contribution. The retailer benefited from exciting promotional activity. The consumer gained through money off, and a value-added offer of free membership to the charity. The business benefited through product differentiation, association with the cause and increased sales.

And yet, despite such a matrix of benefits for all partners, the programme suffered severe criticism. The charity and the business were criticised for the association. It was argued by some that the charity, by tying itself so closely to a particular form of arthritic pain relief, had compromised its ability to provide objective advice on all forms of pain relief. The charity was accused of selling its soul, an accusation that it vociferously denied. The charity and the business partner feel strongly that this was a legitimate relationship that met both their objectives. Additional issues relating to the law in the USA (which led to over 16 states threatening to sue the company), together with media and public rejection of the partnership in some quarters, led to the withdrawal of the programme. Both sides in the partnership nevertheless continued to argue that the programme was, and is, legitimate and appropriate. The question is, who is to judge?

Pre-empting negative criticism

If a risk analysis reveals a potentially contentious issue, it is important to clarify the position of the stakeholders. Indeed, an essential aspect of the initial process should be identifying the potential areas of contention internally (with the partner organisations) and externally (with stakeholders) and being clear where they stand on the issue. Assuming that there is internal and external endorsement for the programme and that all are agreed that the opportunity should be pursued, then a media response should form an important part of the programme. This has been termed the Media Test and is an essential part of the process of developing effective cause-related marketing (see BitC's Cause Related Marketing Guidelines and Adkins, 1999).

There are a number of lessons to be drawn from the example in the case study. Risk analysis is essential, but it is equally important to secure senior internal endorsement of the programme.

Conclusion

There is no reason why all charities should not implement a cause-related marketing programme. The challenge for a charity is to identify what its unique positioning is: what its value might be to a potential partner, expressed in their language, and where, when and how the programme could be developed. All that is required is thoughtful research, planning, targeting, negotiating, imagination and creativity, and thorough implementation, communication, monitoring and evaluation.

So who wins? The potential is there for everybody to win. And how? Through basing the programme on integrity, sincerity, transparency, mutual respect, partnership and mutual benefit and by clear targeting, careful, methodical planning and implementation around a creative idea.

(For a personal view of these issues, from the perspective of the Prince's Trust, see Chapter 11.)

CHAPTER SEVEN

Ethics and standards

Valerie Morton

Introduction

By the very nature of the voluntary sector, ethics and standards have significance for all fundraisers, but they are especially important for corporate fundraisers, both because of the need to balance the objectives of the charity and the corporate partner, and also because of the highly public nature of many such partnerships.

Ask fundraisers what they mean by the term 'ethics' and you are likely to get the 'Heinz' response – 57 different varieties. To ensure full coverage of the subject, this chapter addresses any issue concerning standards and morals that has an impact on corporate fundraisers (for the sake of simplicity, the term 'ethics' will be used to cover all the issues).

A number of the views outlined in the chapter are simply good management practice (in some cases, legal requirements), but some readers may find the approach taken insufficiently 'strict', whereas others may find it too pragmatic. Given the breadth of the voluntary sector, and the nature of each individual's personal convictions, this is hardly surprising and serves simply to reinforce the fact that the subject is likely to generate lively discussion!

The issue of ethical investment has, until recently, been more widely documented than that of ethical fundraising, and some readers may benefit from policies already agreed with regard to investment. Information sources such as EIRIS (Ethical Investment Research Service) can also be useful to fundraisers.

The relevance of ethical issues to corporate fundraising

There are two opposite reactions to the complicated subject of ethics, which may be characterised as the 'head in the sand' solution (ie, just carry on as normal and hope that no one will notice what is going on) and the 'head above the parapet' principle (ie, be completely open about what you are doing, and accept the risks that go with it). It is easy to apply the 'head in the sand' solution, especially when fundraising targets are at stake, but there are many reasons why the 'head above the parapet' principle is not only right, but also cost effective.

These reasons include the following:

- To generate as much income as possible for your cause by both avoiding loss of income (which might happen if, for example, a deal backfired because of the response of either the public or your charity's stakeholders) and also generating new income (for example, donors might come forward *because* of your ethical stance). In addition, having a clear ethical policy will simplify the process of targeting potential corporate supporters, thus improving cost effectiveness.
- To ensure your charity's values are upheld. Charities fundraise only to fund the cause they exist to support: fundraising is not an end in itself. It is therefore not only counter-productive, but also inappropriate, for a fundraising project to contradict the values of your charity. The Royal National Institute for the Blind (RNIB), for example, with its clear service objective to reduce discrimination against people who are blind or partially sighted, would not consider entering a partnership which might result in a negative image of blind people being portrayed. A charity whose objectives include saving tropical rainforests would not enter into a promotion to sell hardwood furniture that used timber from endangered forests. The answer is generally, however, not so simple, so the ICFM guidance note on 'The acceptance and refusal of voluntary donations' (quoted later in this chapter) is particularly useful.
- To avoid misunderstanding with potential and active corporate partners. It is unlikely that any fundraiser wants to have to return a donation or refuse an offer of support – a clear, well-publicised policy should prevent such situations arising.
- To fulfil a responsibility to the sector as a whole. Although corporate partners, and in most cases the public, recognise that each charity is a discrete entity, there is nevertheless a tendency to view charities as a whole, and to ascribe to them certain common characteristics and methods of operation. The activities of one charity can therefore have an effect on the whole sector. A clear policy, reflecting all issues to do with morals and standards, will avoid 'queering the pitch' for other charities.

Defining the issue

Before you devise your ethical policy for corporate fundraising, you need to define the issue by clarifying the subjects that will be within the scope of that policy. You may wish to keep things simple and confine yourself to one key issue (eg the acceptance or refusal of voluntary donations), or you may choose to address the whole range of issues. Be warned, however: the greater the scope, the more difficult it will be to reach consensus on the subjects covered.

In order to identify the issues you wish to cover in your policy, it may be helpful to consider three areas:

The company
- general compatibility with your cause
- nature of products or services
- employment practices
- quality standards
- environmental policy and practices

The fundraising mechanism
- adherence to law/industry guidelines
- nature of mechanic (eg lottery, affinity product)
- associated products (source, safety, etc)
- cost effectiveness (eg what per cent of income generated is going to your cause)

Background and organisational issues
- minimum guaranteed donation
- promotional methods
- use of the donation (eg is it for agreed/budgeted work).

Devising an ethical policy for corporate fundraising

The model that follows shows the eight stages that need to be undertaken when devising and implementing an ethical policy. These stages are:

- research and consultation
- defining the issues relevant to your charity
- creating the policy
- defining procedures
- identifying and creating resources
- implementation – internal and external

- monitoring, evaluating
- revision.

Research and consultation

Stakeholders

Much of the research process has the benefit of both finding out facts and also achieving the important task of consultation. Many of your stakeholders will feel it appropriate to express their views. The information they provide will be valuable; equally important, implementation is more likely to be achieved painlessly if stakeholders have been consulted.

Many charities have a broad range of stakeholders:

- service users/beneficiaries
- intermediaries to the above
- trustees
- individual donors
- corporate/trust/organisation donors
- members
- volunteers
- staff
- purchasers
- suppliers.

It is not unusual for different stakeholders, whether in the same 'category' or not, to have very different views. How are these differing views to be reconciled? Differences between beneficiaries are particularly difficult to address: a charity for disabled people may have some beneficiaries who are willing to support any corporate partnership that raises money because of the use to which those funds could be put, whereas others may not support high-profile money-raising partnerships because they rely on a 'sympathy vote' for disabled people that runs counter to any objective of empowerment. The only solution is to ensure the consultation process is carried out as thoroughly as possible, and, equally as important, that the decision-making process is seen to be clear and fair.

External consultation

In addition to researching external stakeholders (in this case, of course, corporate partners are particularly important), it is valuable to consult any relevant trade association of industry bodies: not only will their input be valuable, but their involvement could enhance the external implementation process. The Royal Society for the Protection of Birds (RSPB), for example, when defining their 'Greening our business partnership' policy, consulted the CBI's

Environmental Business Forum and the International Chamber of Commerce and ensured their policy conformed to guidelines already published by these two groups (see Chapter 12 for a detailed account of this process, pp 112–15).

Defining the issues relevant to your charity

There is an argument for defining the issues relevant to your charity before undertaking the research and consultation process. However, until research has been completed, it is difficult to predict the issues that stakeholders feel are relevant. The solution clearly is to outline the issues in advance, but to refine them with the benefit of the research and consultation. The definition of issues set out above (see p 68) can be used to define a list of the circumstances you wish your policy to cover, some of which are likely to be particular to your charity (eg a charity representing children may not consider it appropriate to include environmental issues unless these have a direct impact on children).

Creating the policy

Creating the policy is arguably the most difficult element of the whole process, because it actually requires making clear decisions. Some of the questions you may need to answer include:

- From which companies, or types of company, will you accept donations/refuse donations ?
- In what circumstances will you accept/refuse donations?
- Are there any fundraising mechanics you will not undertake (eg lotteries, credit cards)?
- Will you always request a minimum donation when undertaking a partnership activity, and, if so, how is this to be calculated?
- Will you require projects to produce income at a certain cost ratio?
- Will you accept funds only for charitable work that has been previously approved, or will you carry out new work if funds are available for that specific purpose only?

It is at this point that personal views can easily come into play. However, it is important that everyone concerned with the process understands their responsibilities in law. This applies in particular to the acceptance and refusal of donations. Charity Commission Leaflet CC3, *Responsibilities of Charity Trustees*, states that 'Trustees must act reasonably and prudently in all matters relating to the charity and must always bear in mind the interests of the charity. They should not let personal views or prejudices affect their conduct as trustees.' It is often difficult for staff, who may hold passionate personal views about various issues, to accept that these views have to be put aside and should not interfere with their fundraising activity. For a more detailed exposition of the legal context to corporate fundraising, see the chapter on the law in the Appendix (pp 148–64).

As an illustration of this point, a number of years ago the NSPCC was offered a promotion involving the sale of fur coats. Many staff felt uncomfortable with the idea and wanted to turn down the offer, some citing their view that the killing of animals for their fur could encourage cruelty to children. However, the corporate decision was to go ahead. Interestingly, although the charity did receive a number of letters of concern from the public, many of these included a donation, because the people writing them understood that the promotion was being carried out because funds were needed.

Defining procedures

No matter how good your policy is, it will fail if procedures are not clear and easy to carry out. The issues you may need to consider here include:

- Who will carry out research on companies, and how will this be done? Research may need to be proactive – and influence the decision of which companies to approach – or reactive – and follow the receipt of, or offer of, support. It is also useful to define the nature of the research required (eg whether it relates to products, employment practices, etc).
- What level of delegated authority do staff have? In which circumstances may they make a decision (because that circumstance is clearly set out in the policy), and when do they need to consult management/trustees? The ICFM guidance note suggests that 'procedures for the delegation of decision making should be established in writing and agreed formally by the trustees'.
- What will the on-going decision-making process be ? Will a committee be created? If so, who should its members be?

Defining and creating resources

It is often tempting to believe (and hope) that an ethical policy for corporate fundraising can be created with existing resources. Although staff time may be available for preparing the policy, there are a number of activities that will require a specific resource allocation, for example the research and consultation process, implementation, any on-going requirement for research, and the evaluation process.

Implementation – internal and external

Once policy and procedures have been agreed, it is easy to think that the main task has been completed. However, without effective implementation, the policy is useless. Similarly, sending a memo with reams of lengthy script and numerous proformas is a sure way to halt the policy's progress (and alienate the very staff who need to use the procedures). You should devise a promotional campaign worthy of the launch of any new product. Your charity's stakeholders are obvious key internal audiences but, if you are to obtain maximum benefit, external audiences such as potential corporate partners and trade bodies should be included in your campaign.

Monitoring and evaluating

Monitoring the policy will not only help you to refine it, but it will also support the implementation process. A policy document is far more likely to be read by staff if their views are genuinely being canvassed. Monitoring should be carried out at two stages: shortly after the implementation, to ensure that the policy is clear and understood; some months later, to discover whether the procedures work in practice. Although it may be stating the obvious, canvass opinion at all levels so that the information is accurate and not just based on what some people think is the case.

Revision

Some revisions may be necessary immediately following the initial launch of the policy. With luck these will be minor, but an initial revision should be considered after the first full year of use, followed by more detailed ones at intervals of two years.

Conclusion

The difficult and sensitive nature of ethics and standards can easily become a barrier to creating a policy for ethical corporate fundraising. However, it is important that all good fundraising managers ensure their charity has such a policy. Not only will it facilitate a consistency of approach, but it will also ensure adherence to legal requirements.

PART TWO

Case histories – the charity perspective

CHAPTER EIGHT

Structuring corporate fundraising

Jeremy Hughes

Introduction

Most fundraising charities recognise funds from companies as a way of contributing to their annual voluntary income. As previous chapters have indicated, securing this income is more complex than simply asking for a donation: in order to earn as much income as possible over the long term, consideration has to be paid to the way in which corporate fundraising may best be structured. This chapter addresses this issue of structure, looking at it in terms of both human resources and systems and drawing on the author's own observations and experience at NCH Action for Children, Muscular Dystrophy Group and Leonard Cheshire and on those of one or two other charities that have kindly shared their experiences. Because the corporate fundraising story is one of mistaken approaches as well as success, the examples in this chapter are attributed to no single charity.

One key point to be made here is that there are no uniform right answers to fundraising problems, and fundraising managers must constantly review their structure in the light of a changing climate of corporate giving and the evolution of their own charity's fundraising.

Moving away from opportunism

Here is an approach to corporate donations with which corporate fundraisers may be familiar:

> A major British company invited two corporate fundraisers to its London Headquarters to make a 15-minute presentation to its chairman, company secretary and two other directors. They were to decide which

charity was to be the beneficiary of their annual £200,000 gift, on the strength of those presentations.

This approach is to be condemned, not because one applicant is bound to be unsuccessful but because it suggests that, even if a corporate fundraiser approaches the presentation professionally, the result is primarily down to luck. Fortunately, cases such as this are increasingly rare; nevertheless, in many charities the belief may remain, among trustees in particular, that the secret to corporate fundraising success is opportunism and personal contact. The reality is that corporate giving is increasingly a result of design rather than accident: the gentleman's club does play a part, but the key is a professional fundraiser working within a structured programme and operation.

A charity employing its first corporate fundraiser is likely to recruit a specialist to work in a central fundraising team. This person increasingly holds the key to successful corporate giving. Fundraisers talk about managing finally to meet the chairmen of large PLCs, only to be told that it is not they who decide which charity to support but the dedicated community affairs team, which operates within a clearly defined, and approved, strategy. This is the team with which the fundraisers have to develop a professional relationship if they are to succeed in securing a donation.

There are two main influences responsible for this state of affairs:

- increasing competition – more and more charities are entering the corporate fundraising market place, but corporate giving has not kept pace with the increasing demand;
- developing partnerships – a one-off donation may be solicited in an opportunistic fashion, but a partnership requires systems and structures if it is to be managed effectively.

Establishing a corporate fundraising structure

The process of setting up an efficient corporate fundraising structure has four stages:

1 Assessing your charity's position vis-à-vis corporate fundraising and devising an appropriate strategy.
2 Agreeing a staffing structure to deliver the strategy.
3 Setting up systems for researching, gaining, managing and monitoring business.
4 Evaluating and, most importantly, reviewing your structure in the light of experience.

The first of these is covered in detail in Chapter 4 (see p 40); the others are discussed below.

Agreeing a staffing structure

The formulation of an appropriate staffing structure hinges on answering the following questions:

- What is your target market for corporate fundraising (eg is it large or small companies? what is the geographical coverage?)?
- What corporate fundraising 'products' are appropriate for your charity (eg cause-related marketing, employee fundraising, donations, gifts in kind)?
- What methods will you be employing to generate new business (eg will it be coming from existing, 'warm' contacts or will it need to be generated 'cold')?

The answers to these questions will help to clarify the skills you will need in your corporate fundraiser or your corporate fundraising team. Thereafter, you need to decide how to distribute these skills. Should every member of staff be able to work with any company and any product? Or would it be more effective to have specialists with certain skills? If you have a corporate fundraising team, or are creating one, should the team be regionally based, centrally based, or a combination of the two – for example, with a central team handling 'product management' or new business?

Central structures can in general be implemented simply and can work effectively. The difficulty arises when you then attempt to lock this into a charity's regional or local operation. Historically, regional corporate fundraising was often undertaken by staff or volunteers seeking one-off funding for a particular piece of equipment or event. It was often assumed that the same resources could simply be tapped again each year. To take one example: a major summer fete was always supported by the local bank, which displayed banners with their logo. The bank had always 'supported' rather than 'sponsored', giving gifts in kind (eg printing) rather than cash. Nobody questioned, year on year, whether another sponsor might offer more, or whether the existing sponsor might be asked to give more.

There are also examples of corporate fundraising being added to the responsibilities of a community fundraiser. This system has the potential to work, but in practice it requires substantial investment and a recognition that the skills and experiences needed to be a good community fundraiser are often not the same as those required for a corporate fundraiser. In addition, it requires very clear lines of demarcation and communication.

Setting up systems

It is rare to find a charity that has kept adequate historical records of corporate giving. In one charity, tidy-minded administrative staff cleared out all the 'old paperwork' belonging to a capital appeal fundraiser when he left on achieving his £1.5 million target. Corporate fundraisers will be used to piecing a picture of previous activity together by trawling fundraising department records, finance department records, reports, minutes, press cuttings and the memories of long-standing staff and volunteers. These last often reveal the most – typically that what appears to be a personal gift is in fact a donation from a company, and vice versa. Commonly omitted from the records are major capital appeals conducted with the help of external fundraising consultants; and yet some of the largest corporate gifts are to be found in precisely this area. Record keeping relates not just to what was received, but to who was instrumental in securing the result. A charity, for example, had cases of company gifts resulting from: an indirect approach via an employee who has benefited from the charity's services; a partner in a leading legal firm twisting a client's arm; and an individual who first supported the charity through Rotary and then took their enthusiasm back into the company. In all these cases, personal contact provided a fertile ground, to which the professional fundraiser had to add the essential ingredients of a well-researched case for support and professional presentation.

This information must be translated on to a database system that, ideally, cross-refers individual involvement to corporate contacts and, ultimately, to corporate support. How to select an appropriate database is more than a chapter in its own right: suffice to say that it is both an issue of system software and the training and practice of fundraisers in the use of that software. The level of investment may be considerable, especially if fundraisers who are based far away from head office are provided with on-line access to a central database.

Issues of responsibility and demarcation

The demarcation issues mentioned above need to be addressed through a clearly defined policy on responsibilities and areas of operation. One fundraiser reports that a major national retailer refused to make a donation because four requests from different parts of the charity all ended up at head office. The retailer told the fundraiser that they did not see it as their job to sort out which part of the charity's work they should support. Another fundraiser discovered that no one was raising funds from businesses in the Doncaster area despite the fact that the city was within easy striking distance of three of the charity's projects: each fundraiser had assumed that another fundraiser covered that area. This is a clear demonstration of how a lack of appropriate systems can lead to lost opportunities.

The simplest way to address this issue is to have a database that identifies key workers for each company and which all fundraisers have to check in advance of any approach. The database can also be used to identify regularly which companies have not been approached, or for which no approach is planned. In practice, because of the difficulties of dealing with brands and subsidiary companies, larger charities with active local networks find that disputes often arise. In such a context, a 'traffic-light' system has resolved the issues. A red-light company may only be approached by the designated head office fundraiser, because there is evidence of major support potential. All red-light companies – of which only the largest charities will have more than a dozen on their list – are maintained as active, current prospects. An amber light indicates that an approach may be made only after discussion and prior approval, thereby ensuring that only the best case for support is presented. Green-light companies are open to any approaches: they are often companies that only consider supporting charitable activity in a very defined geographical area.

The traffic-light system depends on good access to a central database by all corporate fundraisers, and consistent use of it. And, in general, any system will work only if there is trust and transparency between all parties, if flexibility is built into the system and if there is clear direction from fundraising management. Only then can all parties feel that they are being dealt with fairly and that the achievement of their fundraising target is not being jeopardised by other colleagues' determination to meet theirs. Trust and transparency mean bringing people together so that they can get to know each other and talk through any issues of dispute. Flexibility is needed to accommodate volunteers who may unintentionally break the rules but whose enthusiasm and corporate connections need nurturing, not denouncing.

Evaluating and reviewing structure

Successful fundraising has to be responsive to a changing world – changing needs that charities seek to meet, and changing attitudes to giving. Nowhere is this more true than corporate giving, where there is often a direct link between profit levels and charitable support. Any structure for corporate fundraising must therefore be kept under constant review. Although this should happen on a cyclical basis and as part of an overall fundraising strategy, it must also be subject to change at short notice when circumstances dictate. Three such examples might be: when a trend for companies to devolve charitable support from the centre to regional offices is identified, which would require charities to change their structure correspondingly in order to maximise potential income from such companies; where there is a shift from sponsorship support to employee involvement in charitable giving; where a change in attitude, driven by potential market-share advantage as a result of an 'ethical stance', may also demand a review of corporate fundraising structure.

Conclusion

Companies receive many more requests for support than they can meet. They may need to find reason to favour one request over another when there is little to choose between the charity submissions. The experiences illustrated in this chapter show that, where insufficient attention has been paid to structuring corporate fundraising correctly, it undermines the effectiveness of the charity's case: data will be insufficiently captured and shared; fundraisers in different parts of the charity may unwittingly compete against each other in approaches to the same companies.

CHAPTER NINE

Muscular Dystrophy Group – Tesco Charity of the Year

Rachel Billsberry-Grass

The pitch

Like most charities, the Muscular Dystrophy Group (MDG) had long harboured the hope of becoming the charity of choice for a major company and had spent many hours trying to build up links with these companies.

We therefore felt very lucky when Jacqui Ward, a Tesco employee and mother of a boy newly diagnosed with muscular dystrophy (MD), rang to say that, after asking the Tesco Charity Trust for a donation, she had received £500 within a week. She had also been asked to see whether MDG would like to be added to the list of charities under consideration for the 1996 and 1997 Charity of the Year. Of course, our answer was 'yes'.

Soon after this, I was approached by Tesco and asked to submit a written proposal. Before doing so, we needed to undertake some research:

- How much money could we expect to raise as Charity of the Year?
- Given this, which project should we propose that they fund?
- What did Tesco prefer to spend their money on?
- How did they set about raising the money?

The information was gathered from a variety of sources. All the usual books (*The Guide to Company Giving*, corporate directories) were consulted, as was the Internet. We also spoke to past charities of the year and the community affairs department at Tesco themselves. (I am always a bit nervous about doing this, not wanting the potential supporter to get the impression that I have not done my background research. However, provided you have looked at all the information available on the open market and prepared some very specific questions to ask, it is more likely that the company will be impressed by your preparation.)

Armed with the necessary information, we decided to suggest that Tesco fund the MDG Family Care Officer (FCO) service. There were three reasons for this. First, the service is on the care side of MDG's work and matches Tesco's image of 'Every Little Helps'. The FCOs are based around the UK, which worked well: Tesco liked to have a local focus for their fundraising, and it was their staff around the country who would be raising the money, which would then be matched with 20 per cent by the Tesco Charity Trust. Finally, Tesco estimated that the total raised would be around £500,000. We decided to be a little bit more ambitious: at the time, the FCO service cost £640,000 per year.

Knowing how the funds would be raised and that staff were under no obligation to support the Charity of the Year, we decided that we had to include a lot of practical suggestions about how we would ensure the success of the initiative.

The physical proposal was a neat and basic document that used a bullet-point form rather than long flowing paragraphs. I was able to include colour photocopies of some wonderful recently commissioned pictures of people of all ages who are affected by the different types of MD. With the proposal I also enclosed a recent addition to our publications library: an excellent video that managed to explain the very complex conditions of MD and the medical research that MDG funds.

The proposal was well received, and we were invited to make a presentation to Tesco. I decided to take our Tesco contact, Jacqui Ward, with me, since her personal experience of MD meant that she could relay, far better than I could, the value of the FCO service; this would leave me to talk about the support that MDG could give to the stores that would be fundraising.

I believe that Jacqui's involvement was the crucial factor in the success of our presentation. We had everything else in place in terms of what we could offer Tesco, but then so did most of the other charities; what marked us out was the warm and personal touch that Jacqui brought to the presentation. She was obviously not a regular presenter (although still better than many regular presenters), but she was speaking about a subject that was extremely close to her heart: both the slight nerves and the emotional subject matter were evident to the panel, and their empathy was tangible. Add to this Jacqui's status as a Tesco employee, and we were on our way.

At the end of the presentation, we were told we would hear the following week. Jacqui and I agreed not to tell anyone about this, opting instead for 'in about a month' – the excitement at MDG was already too much!

I waited nervously, finding it difficult to concentrate on anything else. The following week, when the phone call came with the good news, I screamed, asked Tesco to fax through confirmation and then rang Jacqui … not much else was done that afternoon.

Planning and building relationships

In May 1995, after we were told the good news that we had been adopted as Tesco's Charity of the Year, planning began almost immediately. In a series of meetings at Tesco offices and at MDG HQ, we established a good working relationship with the Corporate Affairs Department, with whom we would have most direct contact. This gave both parties the chance to ensure that their separate objectives would be met: for Tesco it was important to develop a cross-company fundraising event or promotion that would involve everyone in the company.; for MDG the most important objective was to raise as much money as possible; secondary objectives were to introduce a commercial promotion of some sort and to look for awareness-building opportunities.

During this time we each defined some boundaries. For example, there were some excellent fundraising ideas that had to be abandoned, for logistical reasons that we became aware of only after hearing that our pitch had been successful. Against this, Tesco gave us a number of ideas that had worked well with previous Charities of the Year, which we might otherwise not have considered. It was also important at this point for MDG to advise on how we wanted people with MD to be referred to, for example avoiding the term 'sufferers'.

With the aid of some friendly graphic designers, we developed a special logo for the year that incorporated each of our logos and MDG's mascot, Rupert Bear, who we wanted to be the focus for fundraising. We then set about developing a communications strategy that would ensure that Tesco staff (in Head Office and over 500 stores) and MDG representatives particularly (in 400 branches around the country) would be fully aware of what was going on. Tesco staff and customers needed to know why MDG had been chosen as the Charity of the Year and how the money raised would be spent; MDG representatives needed to know what they could realistically expect from stores and how they could help with the fundraising.

Fundraising mechanisms and support networks

We had known from the beginning that we would have to work for the money. Tesco staff were not obliged to fundraise for MDG, and there was a massive variation in the effort that different stores put into their fundraising, many of which continued to support a local charity as well as, or instead of, MDG. But this was a once-only opportunity and we mobilised or set up various support mechanisms to make sure we made the most of it.

The most important support mechanism was the MDG branch network: there were 400 branches and representatives around the country – many of these representatives had personal experience of MD, and many had been fundraising in their local area for years. They were supported by our nine Regional Fundraising Officers who, as representatives of the local network, were made responsible for day-to-day contact with stores, thus providing stores with that all-important personal contact, as well as giving them a very real understanding of what MD means.

From HQ we prepared fundraising factsheets, easy-to-follow 'recipe' ideas that we hoped would inspire and encourage the Tesco fundraisers.

Like many charities, we already had a range of trading products, many of which centred around Rupert Bear. Warned that the stores would be interested in these products (especially our enamel lapel badge), we established systems to deal with orders from stores and arranged to increase our stock massively. Even so, we underestimated the actual demand for badges.

It was soon clear that our Rupert Bear costume, which had always proved popular at fundraising events with the people attending and with the media, was going to be in enormous demand. We immediately ordered nine more costumes, which then spent the year travelling around the country, stopping off at our offices at intervals.

We set up a 'Hotline' to ensure that Tesco stores could call the fundraising department directly with any queries; we also took on an extra member of staff as the Tesco Fundraising Co-ordinator. The responsibility of the post-holder was to provide a personal, friendly touch for stores phoning in to MDG HQ: someone who would make sure the Hotline was answered quickly and that the stores received any goods they ordered, who would send 'thank you' or 'congratulations' letters and who would try to gather 'soft' information that would give us an indication of the fundraising progress. The position was not simply reactive: in quiet periods later in the year, the post-holder phoned stores to offer support and encourage them in their fundraising.

The Tesco Corporate Affairs Department made sure that we were able to communicate all this information to the stores by including the factsheets, order forms and contact details in a comprehensive pack that they produced. The pack included information posters for staff and customers, blank posters that stores could use for their fundraising events, template press releases, wrap-round stickers for collecting boxes and so on. It also included a special edition of the staff magazine, *Tesco Today*, dedicated to the MDG.

In the course of the year we used a number of Tesco's internal systems, in particular the postal system, to ensure that our communications with stores arrived quickly and safely and at no cost to MDG.

August promotion

One of Tesco's key objectives was to develop a cross-company fundraising initiative, and with this in mind we worked with them during the planning stages and in the early part of 1996, developing ideas to fit the bill.

By this time it was already clear that Rupert Bear was proving hugely popular for fundraising events. As a result, we decided to focus a special fundraising promotion around him for the month of August, the main element of which would be the sale of special-edition Rupert enamel badges. To support this, we prepared factsheets for two very easy fundraising ideas: a Rupert colouring competition and a Rupert Balloon Race. These were added to another comprehensive pack developed by the Tesco Corporate Affairs Department, which included relevant template press releases and details of the promotion.

With the support of Express Newspapers (who own the copyright on Rupert), we provided a cuddly Rupert Toy for each store which could be used as a prize, and special-edition balloons to decorate the stores.

As the enthusiasm built up, some Tesco buyers bought in Rupert products and negotiated with the manufacturers to ensure that MDG received a donation from each sale. We also received small margins from a number of promotional products on sale during the month.

The promotion was an overwhelming success. We sold 110,000 badges in the first week, 260,000 in total: with a profit margin of 85p this was great news! As a consequence, many of the stores increased their fundraising activity and at least 50 that we spoke to afterwards undertook fundraising events when they had not previously planned to. Added to which, the local media loved all the Rupert-themed events, so we achieved hundreds of positive column inches.

Monitoring and evaluation

Since stores were not expected to hand over their money until the end of the year, we had always known that monitoring the success of the fundraising programme was going to be a problem, and that we would be unlikely to have quarterly figures of funds raised, which we would have preferred. Monitoring therefore had to be informal.

Through the personal links established with fundraisers at every level we found out what they enjoyed doing and what was going well, and we were therefore able to keep a rough idea of how the funds were coming in. The Regional Fundraising Officer relayed any event that had proved particularly successful in one area to colleagues, who would then encourage stores in their own areas to adopt the event.

The feedback that we had received even before the August promotion was excellent, and it was clear the fundraisers were enjoying themselves. From conversations with the previous Charity of the Year, Riding for the Disabled, we estimated that our activity was on course to raise a figure comparable to the £850,000 that it had raised.

There is a high risk involved in making forecasts of this type and, in retrospect, this was an area where we could clearly have improved on our efforts. For example, we could have used incentives such as bronze, silver and gold certificates for reaching fundraising targets: the stores would have had to keep us informed of their targets in order to get a certificate – and we would have been able to monitor their progress much more closely.

Income and expenditure

Our accounting year runs from January to December, so the news that we would not receive any money until February or March 1997 was not the easiest thing to relay to our trustees, who were in any case concerned about the time and money invested and the gamble of the return.

Although we only took on one extra member of the team, the impact of the increased workload on the MDG was enormous. The programme affected every department: our post-room staff put in a huge number of extra hours, as did our accounts team, Branch services department, fundraising team and the FCOs. In particular the Regional Fundraising Officers spent much of their time with Tesco stores, which meant that other fundraising initiatives they had planned did not happen.

Having said that, I estimate that the actual cost of managing the programme was not more than £80,000. This may sound a lot, until it is compared with the total we raised – £1.1 million! – and which we started to see from February 1997, with the bulk received by May 1997.

Lessons learnt

This was the biggest fundraising initiative that MDG had been involved in, and almost all of it proved to be a learning experience. There were, however, a few key lessons to emerge.

Our first lesson came early: we had been engaged in excited preparation for months without realising that the most enthusiastic stores would be keen to go for one of the most tried and tested fundraising ideas – selling badges. Before being adopted as Tesco Charity of the Year, our average annual sales of badges was around 10,000. We massively underestimated the early demand from stores and almost immediately found ourselves out of stock, to the great consternation of a number of the stores. Fortunately, they did not hold this against us, and when the supplies eventually came in, three or four weeks later, we sold around 100,000 in the first six months (I try not to think of the extra 30–40,000 more we might have sold).

We also learnt that we shouldn't overwhelm fundraisers with ideas: more is not always better. Most people have been involved in some fundraising before and they know what works for them. As we found with the August Rupert Bear promotion, people will respond if an idea is fun and not too complicated, if the factsheet is clear and easy to follow, and if the idea links with something else.

We also learned to try that bit harder if something at first seemed impossible. Trying to monitor the fundraising of the stores did seem like an incredible task, and we did not try hard enough to find a creative solution. Although we were lucky that no major hiccups were caused by not monitoring progress closely, it would have been easier if we had done so. When we later came to review our year, the solution was obvious. During the planning stages, when everything else was overwhelming and we had run out of creative ideas, we should have called some other charities and asked for their experiences in this area.

Finally, we realised that, while being supportive of fundraising efforts, we should still exercise our professional judgement. The over-enthusiasm of one store resulted in their running a raffle with a car as the first prize – and in my having to prepare a lengthy explanation to the Gaming Board!

All of which leaves only one further prize to mention: the Muscular Dystrophy Group/Tesco Charity of the Year 1996 was the winner of the 1997 ICFM/Professional Fundraising Award for Corporate Fundraising – Most Effective Integrated Campaign.

CHAPTER **TEN**

NFC/RNIB – a moving experience

Mike Lancaster and Hilary Partridge

Introduction

This chapter presents the case study of a very long-term fundraising partnership: the Royal National Institute for the Blind's (RNIB's) relationship with NFC plc, which developed over a number of years and finally resulted in a major Charity of the Year initiative.

The chapter describes the evolution of the relationship from an initial cold approach to the association that corporate fundraisers all strive for – the Charity of the Year – and highlights the impact of the changes that both organisations have undergone; the need to react to these changes and to be continually creative in order to make the relationship work for both sides is also emphasised.

INTRODUCING RNIB

The Royal National Institute for the Blind is the leading charity helping the one million blind and partially sighted people in the UK. It offers over 60 different services from 45 locations across the country. The aim is to meet the needs of every age group through every aspect of life. Services include schools, colleges, residential homes, rehabilitation centres, talking books and much more.

RNIB employs over 2,000 staff, from teachers to braillists, sound engineers to care staff and fundraisers to researchers. It is supported by some 38,000 volunteers involved in a range of activities including reading books on to tape, helping in homes and schools, servicing talking-book machines or raising funds.

Introducing NFC

NFC plc is a leading international logistics and moving-services company. In 1982, NFC was purchased from the UK government by over 10,000 of the employees, who bought shares in the new company, thus making it the biggest ever employee buy-out.

Since then NFC has grown from being a purely UK-based transport company to an international logistics and moving-services company, employing 40,000 people in over 20 countries with a revenue of £2.5 billion per annum. It is listed on the London and American Stock Exchanges.

NFC's operating brands have established operations in North America, Australia and the Pacific Rim as well as in Europe. The subsidiary companies are:

- Exel Logistics, which offers logistics solutions world wide;
- Allied International, which provides a door-to-door moving service across North America, Australasia, Europe and Asia;
- Pickfords, the largest removals organisation in the UK, offering a network of branches.

Turning the key

In 1990, RNIB was in the throes of a major capital appeal – the Looking Glass Appeal. The targets for the appeal were high, with the majority of the income to be generated from support from 100 top companies: NFC plc fell into this bracket, and, following considerable research, an approach was made to the company by the then Head of Corporate Fundraising at RNIB.

In early 1991, shortly after this approach, a link was discovered to James Watson, NFC's Chairman at the time. The link was through RNIB's Director of External Relations, Mike Lancaster, whose visually impaired son attended one of RNIB's Sunshine House Schools in Northwood, Middlesex, where his care worker was the daughter of a personal friend of James Watson. As a result, Mike followed up the funding appeal with a personal letter in support of the appeal to the Chairman in February 1991, in which he asked for a meeting as well as suggesting a visit to the school in Northwood. A donation of £500 was received in the following month from NFC's Charities Committee.

The lesson here was perseverance. While grateful for this support, RNIB felt that there was potential for considerably more support from NFC. To this end, a face-to-face meeting was sought: the conversation in such contexts can be dynamic, and fundraisers are able to get a feel for their audience that enables them to 'sell' their case and make their request for support more appropriately.

Mike therefore thanked the Chairman for his support but repeated his request for a meeting. When this eventually took place, Mike made a presentation detailing RNIB's services and the potential to work together. A number of ideas were discussed, one of which James Watson liked. It was a very simple employee fundraising initiative, which he was prepared to discuss in more detail. A visit made by James Watson to Northwood, where he was impressed by the high quality of service RNIB provides to multi-disabled children, strengthened these links.

Mike's presentation also covered practical ways in which the two companies could work together. The possibilities here included leasing of fleet cars for RNIB employees and the use of Pickfords for removals. There was obviously no pressure from NFC, but, in the light of this presentation, RNIB reviewed their existing arrangements. In the end, however, they decided to remain with their existing suppliers.

Concurrently, another link had developed. Steve Abel, Group Managing Director of BRS (at the time, one of NFC's subsidiary companies), was involved in NFC's Golfing Society, which planned to celebrate its twentieth anniversary by holding an anniversary match from which money would be raised. RNIB was selected to benefit from the proceeds. NFC wanted the money to go to something tangible and visible which was linked to their core business – transport. RNIB therefore selected an ideal project, a minibus for one of its schools.

In the middle of 1992, £22,000 was handed over for the purchase of a minibus. Later that year the Chairman and President of the Golfing Society (among others) attended a presentation held at the school, which allowed them to see RNIB's work at first hand. An additional benefit was that this school (Rushton Hall) was near NFC's Head Office in Bedford.

These involvements strengthened the relationship between RNIB and NFC: the charity had recognised the company's support appropriately, and the company had learned more about RNIB's work by visiting services and talking to RNIB staff.

Changing gear

The foundations of the relationship in place, it was possible to strengthen the links with NFC and to look at taking the employee-fundraising idea forward.

This involved the setting up of a staff lottery, a unique idea of RNIB's. Each employee could buy a minimum of one and a maximum of five chances to win, at £1 per go; the amount was deducted from the individual's salary. The proceeds would then be divided between RNIB and the cost of the prizes, with draws taking place monthly.

As is so often the case, patience is a pre-requisite in corporate fundraising. Things always take longer to set up than anticipated: in this case, board approval for the lottery was received in June 1992, but it was not until the following December, after considerable negotiations, that the plans were presented to key staff at NFC. The launch then took place in April 1993, with the scheme being piloted in their head office with 400 staff.

RNIB attended each monthly draw, which offered a chance to meet and thank staff who were contributing and to tell them more about RNIB's work. On several occasions, short visual-awareness training sessions were run. Through the use of practical exercises, these aim to dispel the myths about blindness and to inform and educate people in how to meet and guide blind people. The lottery gathered momentum over its first year, and it was agreed to extend it for another twelve months until April 1995.

The feedback on both sides was positive. Staff involved awaited the draws in anticipation, and much debate was generated around the offices when the winners were announced. A bit of self-interest combined with a bit of philanthropy is no bad thing!

Freewheeling

Half-way through 1994, both RNIB and NFC saw some personnel changes: a new Corporate Fundraising Manager (Hilary Partridge) was appointed at RNIB, and NFC appointed a new Director of their Foundation. Both were internal appointments who knew their own organisations well, but they needed time to get to know each other's organisation; both also had lots of ideas for change and development.

While decisions were being made on the direction of the NFC Foundation, the lottery continued as agreed, with a review scheduled to take place at the beginning of 1995. In the meantime, contacts developed with visits by the new NFC Foundation Director to RNIB establishments and by Hilary Partridge to NFC sites, to understand more about their business and to identify where the synergy may be found.

When the review took place, the lottery came to an end, having raised over £5,000 in its two years with relatively little effort on both sides. Its success and its potential as a more significant money raiser were recognised, with many discussions about the possibility of extending the idea across the whole company and including more charities as beneficiaries. Given its original involvement and the research it had done into how it could work in a wider context, RNIB had secured its place as one of these charities.

Armed with facts and figures, a joint presentation by the Director of the NFC Foundation and RNIB was made to the NFC Board on the merits of extending the lottery across the business. The decision was taken not to go ahead with the proposal, however: the company was going through considerable change, with new senior management reviewing the structure and cost-effectiveness of the business, and business objectives had to be put ahead of active charitable involvement for a while.

A positive outcome for RNIB was that the board, having seen the quality of the presentation, recognised them as a professional organisation that was prepared to put the groundwork in to make a project happen.

In the meantime, there was another initiative involving NFC's Charity of the Year for 1995–96, Sense, the organisation supporting deaf–blind people. One of the final events of their fundraising year was an Ice Karting Evening. By a further coincidence, this had been secured at a very competitive rate through a contact of RNIB's, so it was agreed that the event would benefit both organisations. The 'Ice and a Slice Evening' took place in April 1996 and raised £2,000 for RNIB.

In the five years since the original contact, therefore, RNIB had received £29,500. Not an inconsiderable figure, given that it began with a £500 donation which could so easily have just been accepted and left at that. This central lesson of perseverance is even more important when considering what was to come next.

Full steam ahead

NFC decided to continue with a headline Charity of the Year: RNIB was delighted to be included in the selection list and to be invited to make a pitch to the NFC Foundation Board for Charity of the Year (beginning April 1997).

Knowing that what the company expects from a presentation is crucial, and, in the light of a rather vague brief, RNIB needed to establish more clearly what the content, focus and tone should be. RNIB talked through plans for the presentation with the new Foundation Director and one of the trustees.

The content put together covered:

- information about blindness
- what RNIB does
- RNIB's financial performance
- RNIB's past experience in employee fundraising

- what resources and fundraising support could be offered by RNIB around the country
- ideas for how the partnership could work
- where the money would be used.

The plans for the presentation also included awareness of the business angle, showing what would be in it for NFC and where the synergy lay.

Mike Lancaster and Hilary Partridge presented on Friday 20 September 1996. Within a few days RNIB received a call from the new Director of the Foundation, Valerie Corrigan, giving the news that it had been chosen as the Charity of the Year. In Valerie's words, the reasons for choosing RNIB were:

> Hilary Partridge made an extremely focused presentation to the Trustees of The NFC Foundation. It was clear that she had a good knowledge of NFC and its operation and had researched her projects well. She had identified where our expertise could be harnessed to design and build a mobile transcription unit for RNIB. It was this in-depth research and the resulting proposed project, which so obviously linked with our type of business, that influenced the Trustees to select RNIB as our Charity of the Year.

The proposed mobile transcription service was a unique and leading-edge initiative. RNIB's current transcription service, which turns any piece of information into the preferred reading format (from braille, to tape, to large print or computer disc), is co-ordinated by several offices nationwide. There is tremendous demand for this popular service which can only be met if organisations are trained to produce accessible information themselves and to provide an on-the-spot service where there is a significant demand. This is what a mobile service does.

In preparation for the launch in April, initial meetings established the nature of the relationship, removed any unrealistic expectations either side might have and clarified terms. The following points were agreed:

- each side's aims and objectives
- the amount to be raised
- whether NFC were aiming to:
  - raise the profile of the company
  - boost staff morale
  - team build
  - increase sales, influence suppliers and customers
  - enhance corporate image
  - provide PR opportunities
- how systems/practicalities would be managed
- how the launch would be handled
- what materials were needed

- what the opportunities were for non-financial involvement
- how much PR support was required.

An action plan was produced by RNIB for internal use, which showed clearly that additional resources would be required to co-ordinate and manage this relationship. It was agreed to recruit a new member of staff, and in February 1997 Karen Hunter joined, taking over the account management of the partnership, with Hilary Partridge as account director.

NFC/RNIB Moving Forward Together

On 10 April 1997, RNIB and NFC launched their Charity of the Year challenge under the banner 'NFC/RNIB Moving Forward Together'. The aims agreed were:

- to raise £200,000 to fund a Mobile Transcription Service for blind and partially sighted people;
- to raise awareness of the RNIB's aims and services.

The NFC Foundation was RNIB's contact for the duration of the charity challenge, with three key members providing the vital link between charity and business and giving fundraising support to NFC staff and pensioners under the guidance of RNIB's Corporate Fundraising department. Karen acted as the RNIB national central contact, liaising with the NFC Foundation, its fundraisers and RNIB's regional network of community and area fundraisers.

NFC nominated 11 regional co-ordinators to manage fundraising activity across the UK. Each co-ordinator was allocated a number of NFC sites to look after in his or her region and was set a regional fundraising target of £15,000 to achieve over 12 months. It was decided that each NFC regional co-ordinator would be given a free rein to manage their area and develop an appropriate fundraising plan.

Similarly, RNIB nominated area fundraising contacts from its team to represent each of the regions. These staff provided a network of local support to NFC as and when required. NFC regional co-ordinators were encouraged to contact RNIB Regional Fundraising if they needed extra support and/or advice, or if there were local events to attend.

RNIB produced a range of specially branded campaign material, to aid fundraising and encourage participation. Materials printed with a joint logo included:

- A fundraising manual, designed to: introduce and endorse the campaign and RNIB; explain the role of the NFC regional co-ordinators; give a step-by-step guide to fundraising, PR, legal and financial considerations; list support materials and provide a list of NFC/RNIB contacts.

- Other materials included leaflets, posters, sponsorship forms, t-shirts, baseball caps, pens and certificates.

General RNIB fundraising support materials were also made available as and when required, and the NFC Foundation agreed to produce materials for fundraising activities on request.

In addition to administrative support, RNIB volunteered to give presentations to NFC groups. The aim of the presentations was to encourage fundraising and raise awareness of the campaign and of RNIB.

A monthly newsletter, produced to act as a fundraising update, was sent to all NFC and RNIB regional contacts; focusing on progress, and on fundraising activities and events, it supported and encouraged fundraisers. In addition, it was agreed that a general meeting would be held every three months to discuss progress and issues.

Meanwhile, each of the 11 NFC co-ordinators set to work planning their fundraising strategy and forming regional fundraising committees.

From the start of the campaign RNIB was keen that a partnership should develop beyond fundraising. It knew that the key to a successful campaign was to encourage commitment from the senior management in NFC. With this in mind, executive fundraising challenges were suggested in an attempt to raise awareness of RNIB among senior members of staff. During the charity year, visits were organised to RNIB service centres, visual-awareness training secured for the NFC Foundation staff, the implications of the Disability Discrimination Act for NFC talked through, opportunities to work together on disability issues discussed; finally, NFC was involved in a number of prestigious RNIB events.

In the development of the mobile transcription units, RNIB was fortunate to benefit from NFC's expertise in logistics: they gave free consultancy on the design and specification of the units and used their immense buying power to influence suppliers. The added value of this support is immeasurable.

A range of other RNIB activities were also heavily promoted. During the year we circulated hundreds of Christmas catalogues, order forms for RNIB's rose ('Perception'), fish-pin badge boards, RNIB service and product literature to NFC managers, staff, pensioners and their families. We spread the word on RNIB, its aims and functions, sold and promoted RNIB products and services nationwide and carried important RNIB campaign messages to as many NFC audiences as possible.

The partnership delivered more than RNIB ever expected, not only exceeding the target but also contributing benefits in the form of substantial gifts in kind such as all the support provided in developing the mobile units. In addition, through NFC's pensioner groups and employees it proved possible to raise awareness of blindness and of RNIB and the services it offers to around 50,000 people. This saw tangible results such as requests for information and advice on different eye conditions, referrals to RNIB services and purchases of RNIB specialist equipment. Finally a lot of people had an awful lot of fun in raising money through a whole range of events.

NFC's view on the partnership is summed up in Valerie Corrigan's words:

> In selecting a Charity of the Year, NFC was seeking not only a 'good cause' but, more, to forge a real partnership with a charity that would ultimately benefit both organisations.
>
> Planning is all-important in a major campaign of this nature, and a joint steering group was established well in advance of the official launch, together with the appointment of NFC regional co-ordinators. RNIB's subsequent appointment of Karen Hunter as our primary contact was instrumental in the success of the campaign. Her constant support both to the centre and the regions was invaluable. It is vital that there is an empathy between the main contacts of the two partners when so much liaison is necessary to ensure a successful campaign: this was certainly demonstrated on many occasions.
>
> Charities can gain more than just money from this type of partnership. NFC took every opportunity to raise awareness among its 27,000 employees and 28,000 pensioners of RNIB and its services. Every opportunity should also be taken by the charity to link in to the purchasing power of the corporate partner where many savings can often be achieved.
>
> The target set for the charity challenge was exceeded, and I am sure that the relationship between our two organisations will continue long after the charity year.

Summary

The following lessons may be learned from the RNIB–NFC relationship:

- Money is rarely given; it has to be raised.
- Money is not offered; it has to be asked for.
- Money does not come in; it has to be sought.

The recipe has been perseverance, relationship building and creativity, mixed with a little patience.

Way back in 1991 RNIB could have been content with £500 and maybe a few similar-sized donations over the years – but it saw the potential and looked for the links with NFC's personnel and/or their business. It worked on involving key personnel, helping them to understand the charity and vice versa, and, despite personnel changes on both sides, was able to maintain this relationship. With this base of knowledge, it was able to be clear about what it could offer NFC and to see the synergy of the relationship, which helped it deliver the goods in the Charity of the Year pitch. Five years may not always be needed to understand a company, but it is crucial to research thoroughly and to understand the ethos and culture of the organisation you are wanting to work with. The other, vital, lesson is not to give up.

The outcome in the case of RNIB – over £230,000!

CHAPTER ELEVEN

The Prince's Trust – cause-related marketing at its best

Manny Amadi and Bert Moore

Introduction

The concept of cause-related marketing (see Chapter 6 for a Business in the Community perspective) might be new to some, but the practice really isn't. Corporations and, most notably, some seriously wealthy philanthropists have been indulging in a form of cause-related marketing for years: Rockerfeller, Carnegie, and Ford (the barons of the American industrial age) set up huge endowments to fund research, galleries, museums, and a variety of social and cultural projects, which originally operated in areas where a more laissez-faire government had no direct interest.

The contemporary phenomenon of cause-related marketing has become more focused. It is less about great individuals and their great ideas, and more about the maintenance of community, the generation of positive public relations, and boosting sales figures. In the last decade, cause-related marketing has been to a very great extent a sales promotion tool. Indeed, it is this incarnation of cause-related marketing to which the public is most regularly exposed, through either affinity cards, or on-pack promotions.

To date about £30 million has been raised for good causes through affinity cards, the recipients ranging from major charities like NSPCC, Mencap, and The Prince's Trust, to arts organisations, football clubs, and trade unions. Midland Bank, the Bank of Scotland, and the Co-op Bank have all launched such cards. Such tools show cause-related marketing at its most basic level.

What has really marked out the modern phenomenon has been the institutionalisation and widespread understanding of cause-related marketing in companies and NGOs: 84 per cent of chief executives surveyed by Business in the Community (BitC) said that they believed in the central importance of business social responsibility, and a large number of companies now boast a dedicated Community Affairs department. Cause-related marketing has been recognised by corporations and charities alike as an effective business tool, a marketing initiative that more accurately reflects the values of the 'caring, sharing 90s'.

How the charity benefits from cause-related marketing

Earlier chapters have outlined the many benefits of cause-related marketing to charities and shown how charities can pitch for much larger sums from the company's marketing budget, if they can think strategically and mirror the aims of the company in question. This opens a huge new funding avenue and often seals a committed partnership for a number of years. There is a great deal that charities can gain from such a partnership: money, certainly, but also the opportunity to learn from and implement the practices of the business sector, and to second staff from the corporate sector. After all, charity is now big business. Recent estimates suggest that 516,000 people are employed in Britain in the voluntary sector, generating between £12 billion and £16 billion each year. Yet there is still a great deal the voluntary sector can learn from the private.

In addition, the PR generated from an innovative cause-related marketing partnership should help to increase awareness of the charity and the work it does. In September 1996, Breakthrough Breast Cancer had the idea of a Kellogg's national breakfast week in partnership with Sainsbury's. Nine million people shop in Sainsbury's each week – a new and captive market for the charity. Partnerships with the corporate sector give the charities the opportunity to speak to a social group that has as yet been untouched and help develop links across all areas of the sponsor company's infrastructure.

Cause-related marketing has encouraged charities to re-appraise the way that they seek funding. It presents the opportunity to be more proactive, and more confident, in seeking corporate sponsorship; it provides the chance to create packages that can be valued in terms of PR – column inches, TV exposure, increased sales and advertising space. In short, it gives the charity the currency of the marketeer.

How the corporate sector benefits from cause-related marketing

Used well, cause-related marketing can build or rehabilitate brands. It can bring the company closer to the community, and to its employees; it can increase sales; and research shows that 8.6 consumers out of 10, faced with almost identical products, will choose the one that supports a charity.

Although the underlying motivation is always reputational, cause-related marketing can benefit business in many ways: marketing, recruitment, employee relations, training, networking, and community relations. A relationship with The Prince's Trust, for example, generates opportunities for a company to both recruit and train staff via the Volunteers programme, which was established to reduce unemployment among 16–25 year olds through the mechanism of community involvement.

The Prince's Trust's national network allows companies to tap into a massive amount of locally specific community work. None of this community involvement is of course entirely philanthropic. Increasingly, companies are recognising the need to bolster local communities in the face of creeping urban decay: as *The Economist* once put it, 'a healthy high street depends on healthy back streets'.

For the corporation, links with 'good causes' help develop stronger one-to-one links with the consumer, thereby taking the relationship on to a 'higher plain' beyond product attributes and lifestyle claims. Identification with positive charities can assist in brand awareness and understanding, differentiate a company from its competitors, even open up new and captive markets. This is particularly helpful for the major British companies and massive multinationals hoping to create a genuine link with their consumers on a more local level: the McDonald's Family Stands at Football, Tesco Computers for Schools (which has provided 34,000 computers for UK schools), or Midland Bank's Student Campaign (with a current market share of 31 per cent) in line with Shelter are outstanding examples.

Finally, cause-related marketing can generate profit: 86 per cent of consumers agreed that when a product or company supports a cause they care about, they have a more positive image of it (BitC/Research International (UK) Ltd, 1997). On-pack links between Daddies Sauce and NSPCC, Covent Garden Soup and Crisis /The National Trust, or Thorntons chocolates/The Prince's Trust have all had a beneficial effect on sales. In the same way, affinity cards of all shapes, sizes, and positive commitments have been proved to encourage a higher rate of spending than those without a social effect. In the main, these campaigns have been successful because the partnerships have properly matched the values of the corporate with that of the charity, what marketeers call 'the fit' (see below).

Planning the campaign

Charity fundraising managers who want partners from the corporate world must be prepared to go out and find those partners, and not expect businesses to come to them. Indeed, they must become as proficient at marketing their organisations as corporations are at marketing themselves. It is therefore vital for fundraising managers to have a well-developed strategy, to know exactly what the nature of the product they hope to sell is – its social, political, and economic advantages to the business world – and to have an approximate programme value in mind. This should be evaluated as any sponsorship programme would be – through an analysis of reach, and of the campaign's marketing strength.

The fit

Above all else, it is essential that charities court private sectors that have a genuine link to the cause. A cause-related marketing campaign where there is not a clear link or 'fit' is very unlikely to achieve its objectives. Frank Bulgarella, a US cause-related marketing expert and veteran of Special Olympics programmes, has no doubt that developing the right partnership is the most important element of cause-related marketing: 'The link of the cause is what makes the sale.' In the USA, where 93 per cent of firms in a recent survey said that they engaged in cause-related marketing, this development of the link has become a marketing art form. American Express has developed a regular fourth-quarter annual campaign called 'Charge against Hunger' – the greatest strength of which is the company's consistency; Starbucks Coffee has produced $20 sampler bags with $2 of every sale going to the promotion of coffee growing in Ethiopia, Guatemala, Kenya and Indonesia. The Prince's Trust, given its emphasis on the 16–25 age group, always seeks partners who wish to make an investment in this area. The Trust works with companies like Marks and Spencer, NatWest, and Sainsbury – who are able both to provide employees for, and also recruit them from, programmes – and is developing a strong working relationship with Sony Playstation, for whom the 16–25 age group is the target market (see below, p 107).

That last example demonstrates one of The Trust's inherent strength in the field of cause-related marketing – the vast majority of its work is with the 16–25 generation, the same youth market that many brand owners find so difficult to reach. This works in The Trust's favour, as does the fact that the vast majority of our work takes place in local communities. The feel-good factor that a corporate donor would hope to generate is therefore fed directly into the lives of the consumers they wish to influence.

10 questions for a charity to ask before entering into a cause-related marketing relationship with a corporation

1   Is the idea you're promoting mutually beneficial? Does it fit into the ethos of both your organisations?
2   Have you got the time and resources to manage the programme properly? Does it bring both of you desired rewards?
3   Can you assure consumers that the partnership is sincere? Does it seem cohesive?
4   Cause-related marketing works on an emotional level. Will your programmes actively engage the consumer?
5   Are the company's senior executives positive about the project?
6   Is the company prepared to devote enough time and money to furthering the project?
7   Have you properly established the parameters of the relationship? ie do you know what to expect from each other? Who is to manage the delivery of programme, media relations, finance, etc?
8   Do you feel that the corporation is eager to involve its employees as well as its suppliers, dealers, franchises, etc?
9   Do you feel that the corporation will give you space to pursue your activities properly?
10 Have you drawn up a legal, binding contract?

Table 11.1 provides an analysis of the key factors for a successful partnership and each party's responsibility for these factors.

Developing and building on partnership

The work really starts once you've agreed upon – and entered into – a cause-related marketing partnership. From the charity's perspective, it is vital to find advocates within your commercial partner. If the company is not engaged both financially and emotionally, the partnership is unlikely to prosper. As with traditional marketing, you should try to find a cause 'champion', preferably at top management level, who has dedicated resources for marketing, public relations and media.

Business in the Community, The Prince's Trust's sister organisation, has developed a Quality Management Model for Business Excellence. The 'Nine

Principles of Corporate Community Investment' listed below, although designed principally as a checklist for the business world, provide a useful framework for the management and development of cause-related marketing partnerships in corporates and charities. If your cause-related marketing partnership can ensure that these principles are being adhered to, the chances are that the programme will be a success for all involved – for the company, the charity and, most importantly, for the beneficiaries of your project.

Table 11.1 Key factors for a successful partnership between charities and corporations

The corporate responsibility of a charity	Key factor for success	The community responsibility of a corporation
– be true to your brand, never sell yourself short – target companies who share these values	'fit'	identify your 'cause heartland' and stick to it
– devise programmes and strategies that involve the consumers, employees, etc (not just tin shaking!)	involvement	let the initiative permeate the organisation (from personnel to technology)
– be sensitive to the tactics you employ	consistency	ensure the organisation behaves consistently with the issue
– provide clear demonstration of the investment of the money received	long term	stay with the issue for the long term (your consumers do); take your time: trust is earned, not bought
– measure the success of your investment in addressing the issue	return	measure the success of your investment against the marketing objectives set

© purple:patch

Nine principles of Corporate Community Investment

1 **Leadership:** the behaviour/actions of the executive team, and all other leaders, establishes corporate community investment as an integral part of company practice.

2 **Policy and strategy:** values and concepts of community activity are communicated in the policy and strategy of a company (ie in annual reports, company memos, etc).

3 **People management:** the organisation releases the full potential of its employees in developing and implementing community programmes.

4 **Resources:** sufficient human and financial resources are dedicated to the project.

5 **Processes:** the quality of corporate community partnerships is enhanced by the right selection of a partner, and through effective relationship management.

6 **Customer satisfaction:** both parties work to satisfy each other's needs.

7 **People satisfaction:** the company works hard to ensure that it is satisfying the expectations of its employees.

8 **Impact on society:** the programme is properly monitored to ensure that it is satisfying the needs of the community.

9 **Business results:** ensure both organisations are achieving their planned results.

Case studies

All this talk of rules, structures, and quality control might give the impression that there is a rigid formula to running a cause-related marketing partnership. The following five case studies of work that The Prince's Trust has undertaken in association with major companies proves that there is a rich variety of mechanisms you can employ under the auspices of cause-related marketing. The Trust has proven very successfully that you can have several partnerships running at the same time, each targeting different audiences with a different partner. The five examples are:

- The Masters of Music Concert with MasterCard
- The BT Swimathon
- The Thorntons/Goldsmiths the Jewellers Diamond Easter Egg Campaign
- *Powersource*, with Sony Computer Entertainment
- Party in the Park with Capital Radio.

The Masters of Music Concert with MasterCard

Background

MasterCard approached The Trust when it was planning its sponsorship of Euro '96 with a very definite objective – to stage an event that would take place in the soccer summer of 1996. MasterCard had a number of more specific objectives:

- extensive, quantifiable and targeted public awareness
- media coverage across the world

- an opportunity for high-quality corporate hospitality.

The Prince's Trust wanted an activity that would:

- generate significant income
- raise the profile of The Trust
- showcase its work to a wider audience.

The event

Summer 1996: 150,000 people packed Hyde Park for the Masters of Music Concert at the height of Euro '96 fever. Rock gliterati Alanis Morrisette, Bob Dylan, The Who, and Eric Clapton ensured national and international media coverage.

Results

The event was a success for both parties. MasterCard achieved the profile to complement their involvement with Euro '96, and had the opportunity to entertain key guests in some style. They reached an estimated television audience of 200 million around the world. Eugene Lockhart, President and CEO of MasterCard International, was delighted with the event: 'The Masters of Music Concert was the highlight of MasterCard's activities in support of our Euro '96 sponsorship,' he commented:

> We were honoured to have the opportunity to work with such a notable and worthwhile charity as The Prince's Trust.
>
> The key ingredients for a successful partnership – including a high-profile, quality event with excellent television coverage – helped MasterCard reach its goal of maximum brand exposure in the UK through the month of June. The Prince's Trust organised the event professionally with a sound commercial approach and great verve. MasterCard was delighted with the results of the project and looks forward to future partnerships with The Prince's Trust.

Well over £500,000 was raised for The Trust. The show also provided a platform for a band formed during one of The Trust's residential 'Rock Schools': Steve Balsamo, the lead singer of the band, went on to play the lead role in Andrew Lloyd Webber's hit musical, *Jesus Christ Superstar*.

The BT Swimathon

Background

BT Swimathon is an established annual fundraising activity with a committed commercial partner. In 1997, The Prince's Trust was selected as its principal beneficiary.

BT Swimathon attracts over 80,000 swimmers from across the country. The event has gown into the biggest participation fundraising event in Europe and has raised over £10 million for 26 national charities. In the UK proceeds were split between ChildLine and the National Deaf Children's Society and the Amateur Swimming Association of Great Britain. The BT Swimathon is recognised as one of the largest community sponsorship events in the UK and is one of BT's biggest opportunities to demonstrate its community commitment through extensive media coverage.

The partnership

It was important for The Trust to consider how it might best support such an established event. One of the Trust's unique selling points (USPs) is its list of committed, hard-working celebrity ambassadors. Trust Ambassadors help the charity in a number of ways, often by meeting the young people The Trust works with and ensuring that The Trust gets maximum publicity.

The pre-event public relations and marketing schedule is a critical part of the BT Swimathon's success. London Events Agency (LEA) Events, who managed the logistics and marketing of the event, worked with the Trust to put together a PR campaign that would attract as many swimmers as possible.

Results

By Swimathon Week, over 33 regional press launches and photocalls and 5 national and home county launches had been organised, supported by over 54 personalities from stage, screen and sport.

The Trust worked very closely with LEA Events to support the PR campaign, both in terms of sourcing celebrities to attend the various launches and providing local information about Trust activities for the regional media. Partly as a result of the involvement of high-profile celebrities and that of HRH the Prince of Wales, the event was covered in 1,536 printed media, on 208 radio broadcasts and 14 television broadcasts.

BT was delighted with the campaign and the media coverage it received: 'We have never had a Swimathon where so many famous faces were involved,' said Rodger Broad, then BT's Community Affairs Programme Manager. 'The Prince's Trust has an amazing currency to offer companies like BT in terms of its celebrity support. Without doubt, it was the publicity and excitement generated by this that helped us to achieve one of our most ambitious targets to date.'

The Thorntons/Goldsmiths the Jewellers Diamond Easter Egg Campaign

Background

The confectioners, Thorntons, had been supporters of The Trust for some years but wanted to organise a promotion that would give them a higher national profile at a very important time of year for them. Goldsmiths the Jewellers came to the table wanting exposure for The Goldsmiths Group name, which was less well known in the UK than their individual store names, and a push on their branding strategy. A desirable partner in the mix and an opportunity to raise funds for a high-profile cause secured Goldsmiths' involvement.

Michael Thornton, the chairman of Thorntons, was particularly keen to come up with an idea that would use his famous brand to raise a significant sum for The Trust.

The idea

The Prince's Trust came up with the idea of hiding replica diamonds in Easter eggs that would go on sale across the nation. The Goldsmiths Group, England's largest quality jewellers, was approached by The Trust to provide the real things. Goldsmiths supplied £25,000 worth of diamonds, and a deal was struck with Thorntons for The Trust to receive 10 per cent of net retail sales from the eggs.

Top celebrity chef Ainsley Harriot supported the launch of the campaign, which ran through the whole Easter retail period, supported by press and poster advertising. The PR campaign was managed by The Trust in close liaison with both partners.

The result

The campaign raised £31,000 for The Trust. All the winners were invited to a presentation at Goldsmiths' flagship store in the City of London, where they were presented with their diamonds by Radio 1 DJ, Simon Mayo, and TV presenter, Anastasia Cook.

'The Diamond Easter Egg Campaign gave great exposure to the Goldsmiths Group name,' said Goldsmiths Group Marketing Manager, Janis Verity. 'It also gave us the opportunity to have all our branches around the UK participate in a national promotion – both core business objectives,' she added.

Debbie Hamilton, Promotions and PR Manager for Thorntons, said of the campaign, 'It not only drove Easter Egg sales, but we achieved national media coverage. It was a good fit with The Prince's Trust, because Thorntons is a family company; its values are similar. The hard work paid off for all of us – it raised awareness of our brands as well as the charity's work.'

Power Source, with Sony Computer Entertainment

Background

Sony Computer Entertainment (SCE) is a perfect fit for The Prince's Trust – it targets its products at the very age that the charity strives to reach with its programmes. SCE came to The Trust with a set of clear objectives:

- to gain a public and media profile by being seen to be giving something back to the community and supporting a charity that helps young people;
- to dispel the image of video games corrupting youth;
- to increase awareness of forthcoming SCE games;
- to form a relationship with The Trust that could be developed in the future.

The Trust's objectives for taking part were:

- to raise £250,000 for a number of specific youth targeted programmes;
- to raise awareness of The Prince's Trust and its activities among the very audience that the programmes are designed to help;
- to establish a lasting relationship with SCE.

The partnership

SCE had a very clear picture of how it could work with The Trust. After meeting The Trust, SCE came up with an excellent plan to produce a special demo disk for the Sony PlayStation at a fraction of the normal cost for this type of product: *Power Source* featured a selection of new games and a competition offering young people the chance to develop a PlayStation video game.

Power Source was sold through the normal retail channels, supported by point-of-sale material as well as press and poster advertising. All the net proceeds from this product after costs were donated to The Trust.

Results

Power Source ended up achieving the financial target of £250,000 set for it by The Trust and went on to reach number three in the games disk charts. The disk featured video footage about the work of The Trust, giving the charity the opportunity to talk directly to its target audience. SCE benefited from its association with a high-profile and relevant charity.

'Sony Computer Entertainment and The Prince's Trust seemed a natural fit for a joint project,' said Alan Welsman, Director of UK Marketing for SCE. 'After all, we are both trying to reach a similar audience and tell them about our products. From Sony's point of view the link was vital in dispelling negative opinions about computer games while raising a significant sum for The Trust. We are delighted with the way the product is selling, and we are hoping we can exceed our targets for The Trust,' he added.

Party in the Park with Capital Radio

Background

The Prince's Trust approached Capital Radio to stage a huge event that would help both partners to build brand image and awareness with a defined target audience. Capital Radio, in the face of aggressive competition from other London Radio Stations, wanted to:

- position itself as the biggest and most relevant radio station in London;
- offer a desirable event to its listeners as a reward for tuning in;
- increase its share of listeners;
- create a strong sense of identity with young people by working with a charity involved in youth issues.

The Prince's Trust's primary objective was to reposition the brand. Specifically, it aimed to:

- present a new, 'trendier' image to a youth audience, moving away from the Eric Clapton, The Who, etc;
- do this without alienating its 'wealthy' donor base of corporations and ambassadors;
- raise over £500,000.

Both partners also wanted to create a joint property that could be rolled out annually.

The event

On Sunday 5 July 1998, 100,000 people filled Hyde Park for 95.8 Capital FM's Party in The Park for The Prince's Trust. Over 20 chart-topping acts – from Natalie Imbruglia, Boyzone, All Saints, Eternal, as well as older performers like Tom Jones and Lionel Ritchie – entertained the crowd. As well as going out live on Capital Radio, the concert was filmed for ITV and international TV distribution.

Results

The concert was sold out in two weeks, which, given the fact that several other concerts/festivals had been cancelled around that time as a result of poor ticket sales, was a resounding success.

The Trust reached its financial target and set a precedent in selling global TV rights for the show. The hope was that this would prove to be a potential source of revenue for future events. In addition, the Trust secured two corporate sponsors – Earthworm Jim 3D and Coca Cola – both of which represented a strong 'fit' for young people.

As far as Capital Radio was concerned, it staged the biggest music event on the summer calendar. Using the concert to offer tickets as prizes for listeners, and hospitality for corporate partners, Capital was able to meet the objectives of 'rewarding its listeners' and position itself as the biggest and most relevant London radio station.

The Party in the Park is set to be rolled out annually – with potential for a huge 'after-market' in CDs, videos, etc which will help to extend the brands of both companies.

Reflections on the case studies

Each of these campaigns had its own identity, and all succeeded because they adhered to these central tenets of good cause-related marketing campaign management:

- each was approached professionally with clear objectives established at the outset;
- a sensible, achievable contract was drawn up;
- both parties stuck to their promises;
- enough time was allowed for the proper organisation and promotion of the project;
- all corporates knew their businesses well enough to be able to give an accurate prediction of income;
- each project was worked on in partnership and had full management support from each organisation;
- the projects were sufficiently resourced;
- the division of responsibilities was strictly adhered to.

The great strength of all these campaigns is that they went far beyond what the conventional understanding of corporate responsibility entails. Sony's *Power Source*, for example, created a lasting product that spoke directly to an age group that marketeers struggle to communicate with effectively; the Masters of Music Concert and The Swimathon allowed MasterCard and BT respectively to leverage the brand and celebrity association of The Trust; the Thorntons promotion produced great PR for the company, which shares many of the values encapsulated in The Trust. All produced a wealth of marketing opportunities.

The construction of well-packaged campaigns has given The Prince's Trust the opportunity to pursue bigger budgets. 'Most companies think in terms of charitable budgets, but we want to get into the much larger funds reserved for marketing and commercial activity,' explains Manny Amadi, Group Development Director of The Prince's Trust. 'Effectively we are competing with advertising and PR to help companies meet their commercial objectives.'

Conclusions

Most marketing messages have little bearing on the real lives of people today and are more to do with what a company thinks the customer wants to hear, than with what the customer is interested in listening to. Cause-related marketing gives the corporate sector the chance to speak more directly to its consumers, to develop one-to-one relationships based on shared values. Cause-related marketing will survive and prosper because it is what the consumer wants – and what the consumer wants the marketeer invariably delivers. (The statistics collated in the BitC/Research International (UK) Ltd's *The Winning Game* – see p 59 – bear this prediction out.)

In many cases, companies choose to pursue cause-related marketing out of pure business expediency, because of its commercial benefits. However, there is now an identifiable trend in the business sector to recognise and pursue more fully its social commitments. More and more this form of 'philanthropic marketing' is encouraging corporations to create their brand identities by playing a leading role in social problem solving – in some respects, by taking over the traditional role of government.

There is clearly a movement developing in which, as Trevor Phillips puts it, 'the values of the sixties become the business of the nineties'. Businessmen and businesswomen have new idols – idols of their youth: Kennedy, King, or Mandela. Contemporary capitalists like Richard Branson or Anita Roddick seem to have captured that caring–sharing zeitgeist. Even in the USA, that beacon of commercialism, men like Ted Turner (with his mammoth $1 billion donation to the United Nations) are promising to usher in a new age of corporate giving, an age that harks back to the business philanthropy of the nineteenth century.

The potent combination of cause-related marketing's new marketability, the desire of consumers to purchase 'ethical products', and the growing social responsibility of business ensure a healthy future for cause-related marketing – a future in which charities such as The Prince's Trust must take a leadership role in ensuring that the campaigns it develops continue to be relevant to consumers, to its target groups, and to the businesses to whom it looks for support. Above all, however, charities need to remember that these campaigns remain only a tool in the service of a charity's objects – in the case of the Prince's Trust, as a means of meeting the needs of disadvantaged young people.

CHAPTER TWELVE

Three case studies in ethics and standards

Case study 1 – Who pays the promotional costs? Reaching a financial impasse

This case study highlights a number of issues relating to standards and ethics in corporate fundraising. In particular, it demonstrates the responsibility a charity has to ensure partnerships genuinely generate support for the charity, and the need to ensure the public understands the nature and value of that support. (Readers should bear in mind that the situation described arose before the implementation of the Charities Act.)

Charity Y was delighted when it was informed by a PR agency that X, a medium-sized retail company, had selected them to be its Charity of the Year. The news was particularly welcomed because it was the staff of X who had nominated the charity, which suggested that a certain degree of support could be counted on from the staff.

At the initial meeting with the agency and the PR manager from the company, it was explained that the company had adopted charities in the past, but that the goodwill of the staff in the previous year had been lost because a number of promises made by the charity – chief among which had been the promise of celebrity visits to each store – had not materialised. In addition, the company was facing a tough financial situation and was, in effect, hoping to get as many benefits as possible from the new charity partnership without having to employ any pump-priming money. To make matters even more difficult, the company expressed an unwillingness to enter into any activity that could negatively affect profit margins. So, for example, most product promotions were ruled out because it would be impossible to guarantee that margins would remain intact.

Knowing how valuable charity adoptions can be, both financially and in terms of profile generated, the charity was determined to develop some ideas that would enthuse the company. The company's main objectives were to improve profile and develop loyalty by involving the customer, and so the charity suggested organising a record-breaking event: income would be generated by selling a series of promotional badges to customers, with the opportunity for customers also to participate in or observe the record-breaking attempt. As

Charity Y had excellent community links, it felt it could organise the attempt with minimum direct costs, although considerable staff time would be required.

The two issues to be addressed were the underwriting of the project costs and the nature and payment of any necessary promotional activity. The charity hoped the company would see the benefits of the idea and could be persuaded to fund the point-of-sale material and offer a minimum guarantee of income to the charity.

Sadly, this was not the case. Although keen to proceed with the idea, the company felt that promotional costs should be paid out of the proceeds of the badge sales. This naturally caused the Charity Y some concerns: although it felt the plan was financially viable, the level of income would be dependant upon the level of support given by the company and its staff, particularly through the selling of the badges. Without a minimum guarantee of income, the charity could be in the position of putting in a great deal of valuable time while facing a risk that the expected income might not materialise. Of equal importance was the issue of payment of promotional costs: if these were to be paid from the proceeds of badge sales, would this be misleading the public, who would otherwise imagine that they were contributing directly to the charity?

Considering all the issues, Charity Y concluded that it was not only ethically wrong, but publicly unacceptable, for the costs of promotional materials to be paid from money given (if not technically donated) by the public. Furthermore, and without a minimum guarantee from the company to indicate its support for the project, the risk of the partnership not achieving an appropriate level of net income for the charity was too high. The charity therefore contacted the company and announced that it was turning down its offer of being the Charity of the Year.

Case study 2 – the Royal Society for the Protection of Birds: an environmental policy for business partnerships

Background

As Europe's largest wildlife conservation organisation, the Royal Society for the Protection of Birds (RSPB) decided some years ago to develop an environmental policy to guide its fundraising partnerships with the corporate sector.

The decision was precipitated by an involvement with an international oil company. A donation had been accepted from the company following assurances that the company would not be involved in any activity that caused environmental damage to sensitive wildlife sites. Unfortunately, just a few days after RSPB had accepted the donation, it emerged that contractors for the company concerned had installed a large pipeline in an area officially designated as a Site of Special Scientific Interest. RSPB felt its only course of action was to return the donation.

Rational for adopting an environmental policy

In the aftermath of this situation, it became clear that an environmental policy should be developed for the following reasons:

- Potential business partners needed to be aware of the environmental standards expected of them before they entered a relationship with RSPB.
- RSPB needed a clear policy to ensure consistency of decision making internally and to prevent personal views influencing what should be corporate decisions.
- As an organisation with almost 1 million members, on whose membership fees the society depended to carry out its work, RSPB needed to ensure that membership income was not jeopardised by any particular corporate partnership.
- A clear policy would facilitate more appropriate targeting of potential business partners, thereby avoiding future controversy.

Devising the policy

In devising the policy, the starting point for RSPB was the principle that it wanted to work with business to further conservation and funding objectives. A number of questions were posed during the early planning stages of the policy.

First, what right did RSPB have to question the activity of other companies? It became clear that RSPB would need to ensure its own house was in order before placing expectations on corporate partners: this was one reason why a 'Greening the RSPB' project was undertaken. In addition to being an obvious step to take in fulfilment of RSPB's own objectives, this measure set achievable standards that RSPB could follow to improve its own environmental performance.

Secondly, should RSPB set up an operation to conduct environmental audits for companies? Although it was felt that companies might expect this of the organisation, it came to the conclusion that, as this service was available in the market place, offering it would not be an appropriate use of charitable funds.

Thirdly, how could the views and wishes of the membership be incorporated into any policy? The simple solution to this was to use omnibus surveys to question members at regular intervals about their views on key ethical issues.

Fourthly, what internal processes would be needed for the efficient and objective implementation of the policy? The processes devised are outlined below.

When it came to devising the policy itself, RSPB liaised with two organisations that were already viewed with credibility by the corporate sector. These were the CBI's Environment Business Forum and the International Chambers of Commerce Business Charter for Sustainable Development. It was agreed that it was appropriate to incorporate the requirements and principle of these two organisations in RSPB's environmental policy, and these became the basis of the policy.

It was also considered important to include four commitments to conservation that companies would be expected to support. Finally, as far as the members' views were concerned, the policy made clear that any link with a business partner should be compatible with the values of its membership.

In order to ensure that companies were clear about the implications of agreeing to abide by RSPB's policy, the final element of the policy covered RSPB's right to dissociate itself from any business relationship should it feel that the policy was being contravened in any way.

The environmental policy is laid out on the next page.

Implementation of the policy

There were three initial stages in the implementation of the policy:

- Fundraisers would use the policy to help select companies that they felt would be likely to endorse the policy. By doing so, they would avoid wasting time approaching companies where there was a high risk that the partnership could not develop.
- Whether the company had approached RSPB, or whether a fundraiser was planning an approach, a request would be made to the co-ordinating member of staff for permission to enter into discussions with the company.
- The co-ordinator would circulate the request to a pre-selected group of RSPB staff, representing a range of interests and experiences in the organisation (in support of the environmental policy, all requests and replies are made by e-mail). The group would be asked to reply within three days, as a reflection of the urgency with which potential corporate partnership needs to be considered. A decision would be based on the outcome of the replies.

RSPB has recognised that it is important to review its policy and processes continually; it is therefore including an additional element to the approval process to ensure a fair and watertight outcome. A select group of six people is being formed to be final arbitrators, should the response from the initial group be inconclusive.

RSPB and business partnerships – our environmental policy

The RSPB embraces two recognised guidelines for the environmentally acceptable conduct of business:

- the requirements for membership of the CBI's Environment Business Forum;
- the principles laid down in the International Chambers of Commerce Business Charter for Sustainable Development.

We ask that business partners abide by these in practice, or demonstrate an agreed longer-term intention to achieve these principles in practice. In particular, we emphasise the following criteria:

- the designation of a director with environmental responsibilities;
- publication of a corporate environmental statement;
- setting of targets for enacting an environmental policy;
- publication of an annual environmental report.

We also ask business partners to support the following commitments to conservation:

- that there is no participation in the destruction of wildlife habitats on land notified as a Site of Special Scientific Interest (SSSI), an Area of Special Scientific Interest (ASSI – in Northern Ireland), a Special Protection Area (SPA), a 'Ramsar' site, or candidates for such designations, as well as protected land outside the UK;
- to actively avoid any adverse impact on bird species specified on the 'red' or 'amber' listings in the UK Biodiversity Action Plan;
- that all UK and EU legislation designed to protect wildlife is upheld;
- that there is no involvement in directly passing technology agreed as environmentally unsound to developing countries.

Our business partnerships are initiated with the best intent and on the basis of mutual understanding. However, situations may arise in which a link with a current or prospective business partner could be seen as incompatible with the spirit of RSPB's conservation mission and its membership.

In such instances, every effort will be made to achieve a mutually acceptable solution, but the RSPB must retain the right to disassociate from a business relationship and comment on the circumstances as necessary.

Case study 3 – an ethical conundrum

Background

This case study concerns a development agency, whose principal mission was to remove from places of war and danger refugees (particularly children and women) who, through no fault of their own, were placed at risk by the fighting. The case in question occurred in the countries of former Yugoslavia, at a time when some of the most ferocious and horrendous incidents were taking place, and when 'ethnic cleansing' was being carried out by some of the warring factions.

Like many other development agencies, this particular agency had a well-established ethical policy in respect of receipt of support from commercial organisations. After broad and public consultation with its supporter base, the organisation had established the principle that it would not seek, or receive, support from commercial organisations that were involved in the armaments industry. The justification for this position was that the objects of any armaments company were antithetical to the core object and mission of the agency.

A problem requiring an immediate response

As part of its work in the former Yugoslavia, the agency was at the forefront of efforts to remove from areas of enormous danger and terror those refugees who, by virtue of their ethnic minority status, were being subjected to intimidation and physical abuse. One particular group of refugees, trapped in one of the more remote enclaves, had deservedly achieved considerable media attention and there was great concern for their future well-being, indeed for their very survival. The charity was making great efforts (covered on the television screens of countries throughout the world) to remove these refugees to a place of safety. However, the geographical remoteness of the enclave and the nature of the terrain between the refugees' point of siege and the sanctuary of the UN lines meant that the efforts of the agency had thus far been without success. The only vehicles able to effect the safe transport of the refugees from the enclave to the sanctuary were a particular type of armoured carrier which the charity had neither access to nor the resources to purchase. It was quite clear that this desperate situation would be resolved, positively or negatively, within the following 48 hours.

A knight in tarnished armour

At this time of considerable stress and turmoil, when the actions of the charity itself were under intense media scrutiny, a commercial organisation offered to provide a fleet of six such armoured carriers within a 24-hour period to enable all the refugees to be transported safely and securely outside the enclave.

Acceptance of this donation, which the company offered with only one stipulation, would have enabled the charity to achieve its charitable objects and mission and remove all the refugees from their place of danger. Failure to act, and to act quickly, would almost certainly lead to the death of the refugees.

However, the charity's Director of Fundraising was faced with a particular ethical dilemma that was a result of the nature of the company concerned and the stipulation that the company was attaching to the gift of the armoured carriers.

The company concerned was an armaments company. Not only was it an armaments company, but the very equipment being used by the warring factions in former Yugoslavia was certain to have come – in part at least – from the company itself. Further, in offering to donate the armoured carriers, the company had stipulated that each of the fleet of armoured carriers must have the full company name and company logo emblazoned on all sides of the truck. This stipulation was clearly made in the knowledge that media coverage of the refugees' evacuation would achieve prime-time television coverage throughout the world.

Resolving the dilemma

So, what was the Director of Fundraising to do? On the one hand, the charity could accept the gift and thereby – possibly *only* thereby – ensure the evacuation of the refugees and the achievement of the charity's mission; but the charity could only do this by disregarding its ethical policy, formulated with the full agreement of the charity's existing members (who were supporting the work of the agency in the enclave), not to accept support from armaments companies. On the other hand, the charity could refuse the offer of support, thereby complying with the ethical code of practice agreed with its supporter base; but in so doing it would expose to continuing danger and possible death the refugees whom the charity existed to help.

The Director of Fundraising contacted the Institute of Charity Fundraising Managers (ICFM) and asked for advice and guidance on the practical course of action that he should take. The ICFM's advice was that the charity had no option but to accept the support, since the organisation would otherwise not be able to address its core mission. The charity wrote to all its existing supporters explaining the dilemma it faced and indicating why it had taken the action it had. Although this was not intended as a fundraising appeal, the letter raised more money than any other previous appeal.

CHAPTER THIRTEEN

Managing gifts in kind

Jon Scourse

Introduction

We often think of corporate giving purely in a financial context. For most charities, funding is the key issue and it is logical to pursue donations using the various routes into corporate budgets. However, most companies can give a great deal more. Traditionally, secondment of staff has been a powerful ingredient of corporate support, but what about all the other aspects that are so often overlooked? Approaching companies with an open mind and with the ability to think laterally can yield surprising results that can be of enormous value.

'Gifts in kind' is a broad description that in itself needs qualification. Leaving aside secondment, which is a form of gifts in kind, this form of giving is commonly associated with material goods. This chapter will demonstrate, through the specific example of one charity (Children's Aid Direct), how services can be of value to the voluntary sector as well.

What do we understand by gifts in kind?

There are three main elements to gifts in kind:

- Material products that are of direct benefit to the charity and assist it to do its work more effectively, for example the donation of a truck to Children's Aid Direct by TNT or the provision of used office furniture by local companies.
- Material products that can be used by the beneficiaries of the charity, for example quality-control rejects that are basically sound but unmarketable for superficial reasons such as faulty labelling. Sometimes this can be used product that is still of enormous help when correctly targeted: for example, Eurocamp has donated over £1 million worth of products for use in Albania and Bosnia.

- Service provision by companies. Most major companies have developed their own specialist service providers that can be accessed for the benefit of staff and recipients: for example, Yellow Pages provides free training to Children's Aid Direct staff when spaces are available on its own staff development courses.

Children's Aid Direct has developed a strong relationship with many companies based on the provision of donated aid given as gifts in kind. Since 1990, over £15 million worth of such aid has been distributed to children and their carers, particularly in Eastern Europe. As evidence of the value of this support, Children's Aid Direct is one of the leading UK charities in terms of gifts in kind.

However, it must be understood that donated aid was a part of the ethos of the organisation since its foundation as Feed the Children in July 1990. From the earliest days, companies were approached to provide materials for onward distribution by the charity staff using their own transport fleet. The organisation operated as a transport and logistics specialist that bridged the gap between the provider of aid and the real emergency need in the field. In this way, the donor company really felt involved and could see that their contribution made a difference – feedback by field staff is always critical.

The charity's attitude to gifts in kind has shifted over the years, and it has come to realise that there are many strategic issues that can be very costly if not carefully considered. Any charity contemplating gifts in kind as a major initiative needs to be aware of these risks, which the next section shall now outline.

Strategic issues

Donated product – can you afford it?

By definition, any gift in kind for use by beneficiaries requires distribution – which means costs. If this can be handled locally using volunteers, costs can be kept within reason, but, if the work is more complex, gifts in kind can be an enormous drain on financial resources. Either way, gifts in kind will incur costs of warehousing and storage, staff and security, transport and appropriate administrative controls. This is particularly the case for overseas aid as there are usually complex customs procedures and even duties to pay. For smaller charities, finding such funds to maintain such an operation may be difficult; it can be easy to accept donated products without considering these implications. It is therefore critical to make provision within budgets, but if the donor company can be made to appreciate this factor and either assist directly with distribution or make an added financial contribution, this is desirable. Experience suggests that, when a company offers products that may be worth many thousands of pounds, they are surprised to be asked for funds as well. The tactful explanation that this necessitates can sometimes open the door to wider support by involving staff in activities to raise funds to enable the delivery of goods supplied by the parent company.

This contrasts directly with gifts in kind that are for direct use by the charity and which are primarily providing added value to the operation.

Is it cost effective?

Directly linked to the above is the question that any charity accepting gifts in kind for recipients must ask itself: is it cost effective? If the cost of distribution exceeds the value of the goods, then how can it be justified? It is likely that only in extreme circumstances would the value in non-financial terms justify the costs if the financial worth of the goods is low. For instance, plastic sheeting for refugees facing winter in life-threatening conditions is entirely justifiable, although the cost of distribution will probably exceed the value. However, the question that must be asked before the gifts in kind are accepted is this: can we purchase these goods locally or regionally ourselves? If the answer is 'yes', it will cost less in the long run because transport and distribution costs will be reduced. As a rule of thumb, serious questions should be asked if the costs of handling the gifts in kind exceed the value of the product.

Although Children's Aid Direct works currently in nine countries, gifts in kind are generally only distributed in Eastern Europe. This is for two reasons. First, it is simply not logical, in terms of cost and time, to transport materials across larger distances to, say, Africa (although the charity is currently evaluating the use of containers for direct delivery from the UK of items that are not available locally). Secondly, we have to consider local cultures, and for many areas the products donated would be inappropriate. For instance, a donation of baby clothes for the UK market would be of little use in equatorial Africa, but of great value to mountain communities in Albania.

Matching needs with donations

It is very important to match the needs of the recipient with the type of product being distributed. These needs have to be thoroughly researched in the field. For this reason, it is important that the process is donor led: only by then determining what is appropriate should aid be accepted from appropriate sources. Many donor companies make *assumptions* about what is needed, which can lead to the wrong goods being distributed at enormous expense when they are not even needed, if the charity handling them is not well disciplined. There have been many examples of this, particularly in Eastern Europe. Charities must be prepared to reject an offer of goods unless it clearly meets the above criteria.

There is also a risk that unscrupulous companies may 'dump' a problem product by donating it to a charity: this is particularly likely when 'sell-by' dates are an issue. Great care is needed to ensure that charities are not exploited in this way. In one case, a truck arrived at a charity's warehouse without informing the charity and dumped medical products that turned out to be very close to their expiry date and would have been dangerous to use. No paperwork was given, and the charity had to dump the entire load at its own expense.

Unless a charity is directly concerned with medical aid and has the appropriate skills and experience, donations of medical products should always be rejected. Hygiene products and non-prescriptive medicines are acceptable, but only if extreme care is applied to the process whereby they are donated.

The same caution may be extended to other areas, particularly to technical products. In the early 1990s, sending donated incubators to Albania was considered a good idea, until it was realised that people had neither training in their maintenance nor access to spares. Providing the back-up services as part of the package was beyond the skills and remit of the original donor charity: as a result, this well-meant initiative was not sustainable.

Is it in the best interest of the recipient?

During an emergency such as the war in Bosnia, donated aid can be critically important and can save lives. For the duration of this war, Children's Aid Direct actively sought and accepted all sorts of product – from seeds and tools, food, hygiene products, children's shoes, blankets, chocolate, to toothpaste. Hundreds of companies were approached, and over £20 million worth of aid was distributed.

Once the emergency phase ends, and the economy begins to recover, the charity is soon faced with a dilemma. A judgement has to be taken that reflects the need to assist the population to recover by providing not aid but the expertise and raw materials to assist people to re-build their lives. Local markets are a critical part of this process but are very delicate at this stage. It is therefore unhelpful to deliver truckloads of goods that will actually deny the local recovery and may even create a culture of aid dependency. This is a difficult change to manage: with Children's Aid Direct, this has led to a thorough review of its activity and even closer scrutiny of the type of aid offered and the regularity of its delivery.

Implications of accepting gifts in kind for recipients

The discussion of costs so far has referred to having the correct structures in place in order to handle the gift. By accepting the gift, the charity is accepting responsibility for a distribution of the gift that must meet the donor's expectations as well. Donor companies also have concerns about how their product, and particularly their brand, is used and are very sensitive about security. For this reason, some companies favour an overseas operator that can specify a country where there is no established market for their brand. For instance, Children's Aid Direct accepted Johnson & Johnson products for babies, but on the understanding that they will be sent to Bosnia and rural Albania only. Major brands are justifiably concerned that any large-scale donations are potentially damaging in the wrong hands.

For these reasons, the charity becomes, functionally, a distributor of goods. This has serious implications:

- Staff will be needed to look after paperwork (especially for customs, etc) and security.
- Staff or volunteers will be needed to pack the goods and distribute them onward.
- Secure warehousing will be required: shared warehousing is a huge risk.
- Secure secondary warehousing is needed as well, unless the goods are to be distributed directly.
- Transport will be needed, which may be donated as another gift in kind; however, serious players in gifts in kind will need to expend funds on their own fleets or reliable contractors.
- Systems are needed to ensure direct and secure delivery to the final recipient; by their nature these systems are laborious if security is to be ensured, and they require close monitoring.

Donor expectations

If a donor company is providing gifts in kind of high inherent value, it has to be confident that the product is in safe hands: the recipient charity must be able to demonstrate this. Providing evidence of distribution can be an enormously powerful tool for the corporate fundraisers, and some of the best long-term relationships are made from this start: actually being able to visualise the difference that their products make is a powerful message that motivates staff at all levels.

The importance of giving feedback to donors, even when it has not been requested, applies especially to gifts in kind, even if the donation is for direct use by the charity.

Evaluation

Gifts in kind require considerable investment, and the opportunity costs of the time spent searching and locating product gifts must be considered. Determining the value of goods is difficult, but the donor company should be able to indicate a book value of the donation. However, evaluation needs to be handled with care, because this value may reflect an ex-factory price and not the full retail value. Accurate records are also needed to cover issues of insurance: in the case of overseas aid, these values are needed for customs clearance in any case.

The value of gifts in kind may justifiably be treated as a form of income, when it is considered that resources are required to generate gifts in kind as much as to generate other forms of support.

Further development

Widen the relationship

Many companies prefer the tax-efficient route of giving material, but the real benefit to companies can lie in the donation of goods that have already been written off, which enables the donor company to provide assistance of a high value to the recipient at only marginal cost – such donations can then be valued as a corporate donation.

Companies that donate products can be encouraged to take on other activities, if care is taken to build a relationship with them and to provide them with feedback on their donation. Photographs of donated product being used effectively usually merit a feature in the in-house publications and can arouse interest across a company. This, in turn, can be turned to advantage and lead to the development of staff fundraising, donations and payroll giving: the next logical step would be for the company to adopt the charity as its Charity of the Year.

Staff involvement

Donated aid can offer the opportunity to involve staff in a practical way, most obviously in its distribution. This can develop high levels of staff morale and result in high-quality volunteer input: such individuals can then act as ambassadors within the company with possible influence over the charity decision-making process. Staff at Yellow Pages in Reading have dedicated entire weekends to pack aid for Children's Aid Direct as part of a structured support programme organised by the parent company.

Case studies

Granada television appeal

Although not strictly a corporate scheme, this appeal demonstrates the problems that can occur with gifts in kind if they are not carefully controlled. During the early stages of the war in former Yugoslavia, a Granada TV team reported from the frontline on the work of Feed the Children (as Children's Aid Direct was then known). This resulted in an appeal for viewers to donate food packages for refugees in Croatia for distribution by the charity. Red Star Parcels agreed to transport the aid free of charge to Reading.

As the charity had not undertaken an aid programme of this kind before, it was difficult to forecast the uptake of this appeal. In the event, the response exceeded the expectations of the charity and stretched its resources to the limit. The need to fund this level of activity had not been anticipated, and the result was a major logistical and cash crisis for the charity that threatened to overwhelm it. The response was so great that the Reading depot reached capacity, Red Star had to use Euston, and Feed the Children had to fund further warehousing, extra staff and many more trucks than budgeted. The crisis was averted, but largely because of the timely intervention of Virgin Atlantic with the loan of a 747 jet.

The lesson from this case study is never to accept donated gifts unless you have the financial and logistical means to handle them.

Clarks Shoes

In 1992, Clarks Shoes approached Feed the Children with the offer of a scheme to collect used children's shoes in selected stores. Parents purchasing a new pair of shoes were invited to donate the used, out-grown pair that would otherwise have been thrown away. Operating at the point of sale, this scheme captured the attention of Clarks customers: since the company is the leading UK supplier of children's shoes, the scope was enormous. The shoes were collected by the company as part of the standard distribution network to the Somerset headquarters, where the charity organised one collection on a regular basis. They were then checked by volunteers at the Feed the Children warehouse to ensure that only good-quality products were distributed. This simple mechanism has enabled the distribution of over 900,000 pairs of shoes to children to date, particularly in Eastern Europe. In the course of the war in Bosnia, Gordon Bacon, the Country Director, said:

> The formula is very simple. Without shoes children cannot get to school; without school there is no education; without education, no future.

As the situation in former Yugoslavia changed, shoes ceased to be a priority, and the collection has now been discontinued: gifts in kind must always be appropriate to the needs of recipients, and in most cases they will reach a point where they are no longer effective.

The relationship with Clarks Shoes has since broadened to include staff activities and sponsorship of the Three Peaks Challenge, which in three years has raised £340,000.

Eurocamp

Eurocamp is the leading self-drive camping holiday operator in the UK. Family holidays are marketed on the basis that equipment is usually no more than two years old. This prompted Children's Aid Direct to approach Eurocamp to seek products that were surplus to requirement. Since 1993, the value of donated goods has reached £1 million, with products proving to be of enormous value in human terms: hundreds of tents were distributed to refugees in the Bihac area of Bosnia in the 1994 winter; 1,600 refrigerators have been distributed in Albania, primarily to child-based institutions such as schools, homes and hospitals; 10,000 sets of plastic furniture have reached schools throughout Albania. Perhaps the most successful item has been mattresses that were found to be ideal for the creation of play areas for disabled children who would otherwise have been confined to their cots.

The relationship between Eurocamp and Children's Aid Direct has also been developed, so that Eurocamp now has a feature in its catalogue which is marketed directly to 300,000 customers. Staff have also been active as fundraisers.

Conclusions

- Gifts in kind destined for use by beneficiaries need careful management and, to succeed, must be included in the strategic planning of costs and resources.
- The gift must be appropriate to the need. Care must be taken in dealing with donor companies.
- Evaluation, security and control can be difficult.
- Gifts assist the charity to develop a wider relationship with the donor company that can be mutually beneficial.

PART THREE

Case histories – the company perspective

CHAPTER FOURTEEN

Developing a CCI strategy – a case history from BT

Stephen Serpell

The business context

For several years, BT has operated the nation's most extensive corporate community programme. This is a challenging role: cast into a leadership position, BT is deeply concerned to lead well. Sir Iain Vallance has made clear BT's attitude to its community programme:

> To some degree, we do it because we are that kind of company. But, we wouldn't do it if we were not convinced that this was a two-way street, where everyone concerned could benefit and where the benefit was tangible and visible.

BT's community activities therefore not only reflect its commitment to good citizenship, but also directly assist BT's public standing and reputation, which BT regards as one of its strategic commercial assets. The company is very conscious that people do not just 'buy' products; they also 'buy' the organisation behind the product. BT would like its reputation to be such that governments as well as customers want to do business with the company and want it to succeed, that good potential employees want to join it, and that existing employees are proud of it. BT's Community Partnership Programme is therefore not just philanthropy, but a measured investment that can, and should, be justified to all the company's stakeholders.

History and approach up to 1995

As a founder member of the 'Per Cent Club', BT has consistently set aside at least half a per cent of its pre-tax profits for community causes (as defined by Business in the Community), which in 1996–97 amounted to £15 million in the community programme. It should be stressed that this does not include the costs of other community contributions such as TypeTalk (a telephone service for the deaf), Talking Telephone Directories for the Blind, 999 Services, or Malicious Calls Tracing; a recent assessment using the London Benchmarking Group method estimated an overall community contribution by BT of almost £30 million. However, because the resource is spread across a number of areas – including education, economic regeneration and the arts – only a fraction of the total has ever been available for external charities.

Up until 1995, BT divided its support between six separate areas, which enabled the company to assist an exceptionally broad range of activities. From some points of view, however, the programme was more philanthropic than it was effective: its huge portfolio of over 150 projects meant that its impact was very diffuse, and, despite its size, the overall programme seemed to garner very little recognition. Projects were often simply responses to unsolicited proposals from community organisations (BT receives up to 80,000 of these each year), and management was split between three different departments. This prevented any effective synergy and gave the whole programme a reactive stance, which demonstrated no particular connection with BT's mainstream activities. There was a perception, too, that some of the beneficiaries were beginning to take BT's contributions for granted and that the company was seen in some quarters as a 'soft touch', a combination that devalued the process for both sides.

Strategy development

These issues were tackled in a strategic review in 1995–96, which led to an updated mission statement for the community programme, new objectives, a guiding theme, and fresh project selection criteria.

The change to the mission statement was striking. Previously, the programme's main direction had been drawn simply from one of BT's overall corporate aims: 'to make a fitting contribution to the community in which it conducts its business'. A far more focused role was now defined for the community programme, maintaining the old goals but additionally emphasising relevance to the company. The new mission statement reads:

> BT is committed to a programme of investment in and partnership with external organisations which: demonstrably improves the quality of life and well-being of the communities in which BT operates; builds and maintains the company's reputation; provides a source of pride in the company for its employees and a means for their involvement and participation in the community; and enhances BT's business.

The aims of the programme were also expressly linked with BT's 'corporate scorecard', a strategic tool now used in many companies to ensure the consistent and balanced setting of objectives for the entire business. Application of the 'scorecard' was therefore a radical step, which firmly embedded the community programme into BT's overall direction-setting process. The resulting objectives included demonstrating high levels of community satisfaction as measured by external surveys; communicating clear, positive messages about BT; and substantially increasing the number of BT people actively assisting the community.

BT also wanted to improve its focus by adopting a unifying theme to articulate all its community activities. This was perhaps the most difficult and carefully discussed part of the whole strategy review. Having a theme – which had to be clearly relevant to BT and fit the company's key strengths in communications, national reach and technology – was seen as a way of being more proactive about the programme, taking control of its agenda instead of just responding to external stimuli.

In the end, BT adopted the issues of access and communication and, specifically, the guiding theme of 'communications skills', which provided a good fit all round, linking well with the human as well as the physical factors of communication, which are a particular focus for the company. The theme also formed a natural progression from the community programme portfolio as it then stood.

Existing areas of involvement outside this immediate focus were not perceived as a problem; the company would certainly stand by all its previous commitments, but would not renew or extend its role in projects where relevance to BT was too tenuous.

The new programme

In the wake of this work, BT restructured its community programme, bringing it into a single department with just three sections. New selection criteria came into force, which looked for:

- genuine relevance to BT;
- demonstrable benefits to the community, the delivery of which may clearly be established;
- clear communications plans to ensure visibility;
- an expectation of positive support for BT's reputation by project partners;
- increasing involvement by BT people;
- for a proportion of cases, attested enhancement of BT's business (for example in cause-related marketing projects).

It should be stressed that not all projects have to demonstrate all these criteria, but they must demonstrate at least some, and the programme overall is judged internally by how it delivers on all the criteria.

The programme also started to take an increasingly proactive line with charities, seeking to focus resources on specific issues related to BT's guiding themes and strengths. One effect of this was to introduce one large award scheme to back charitable work on interpersonal communication, and another to back projects that depend on communications technology. Together, these received several hundred applications and led to ten partnerships with organisations, to which BT contributed about £100,000 each – but on the basis of much clearer expectations about deliverables, as well as support for BT's reputation, than before, and with a clear plan to benefit not just from BT's money but also from its particular areas of expertise.

A clearer view of community expectations

These changes have given BT's community programme much better focus, but the company has continued to refine its approach.

The next major step was to re-visit the extent to which the programme aligned with the wishes of BT's stakeholders. The 1995–96 strategic review had relied rather heavily on developing best practice with advice from consultants and from various panels, including a long-standing community liaison panel of voluntary-sector representatives. By 1996–97, however, BT had consolidated the results of a number of substantial, statistically valid surveys of each of three key stakeholder groups:

- opinion formers (leading figures in public life)
- the public (which, for BT, also provides a good measure of the view of its customers)
- BT's employees.

In each case, BT obtained survey data not simply on what the group felt that business in general should do to support the community, but explicitly on what it felt BT should do. The surveys also checked on the level of awareness of BT community activities, and on the level of approval attached to these.

Perhaps the most significant outcome of these surveys was the identification of each group's priorities for BT. The 1996 surveys showed clearly that the greatest area of concern was a cluster of issues to do with employability – such as education, training, and life skills – together with a strong desire for BT to help in the community on matters of health and welfare. The surveys also revealed a positive expectation that BT should support causes that are relevant to its business.

BT is now updating these surveys on a regular basis, and is using them to guide its community activities within its overarching theme of 'communications skills'. The 1996 findings underscored the importance of BT's existing community work in the education sector, but they also focused on projects that assist people's employability, either directly through education and training, or indirectly through health and welfare initiatives that in turn enable people to move towards self-sufficiency.

These changes have all tended to move BT towards a programme that is not just increasingly proactive, but increasingly issue centred. BT's multi-million pound contribution to the community is of a size comparable with a leading national charity. It has traditionally distributed this resource very broadly; but its increasing focus could enable it to make a significant difference on some specific social issues, if it chose to do so, in conjunction with the right strategic partners in the voluntary sector. This is illustrated by the company's very large initiatives in education, public fundraising and volunteering for the Millennium, all addressing aspects of 'communications skills' and centred around its major 'FutureTalk' campaign.

All this means making a difference and not just making a contribution.

Measuring the difference

BT's particular interest in assessing the impact of corporate community programmes has been prompted to some extent by its association with Total Quality Management (TQM) and the associated Model for Business Excellence (see p 101), which is used by hundreds of companies across Europe as a tool to assess the quality of their overall business. The Model is owned by the European Foundation for Quality Management (EFQM), and it requires companies to assess themselves against nine headings, one of which is 'Impact on society'. The methodology is demanding, and requires quantitative, objective data on social impact, evidence of a well thought-out approach, and results that show improvement over time. Independent external assessment is available and results in banded scorings. The significance of this model is not to be understated – you cannot be a 'total quality' company without using it.

BT has taken the step of freely publishing its 'Impact on society' chapter, and in 1997 assisted Business in the Community to develop the EFQM Model into the new set of Guidelines for Corporate Community Investment. Business in the Community launched these new guidelines to the members of the Per Cent Club in July 1997, and there is strong international interest. BT remains heavily involved in assisting the further development of assessment and social reporting methods.

Conclusion

BT has a very large community programme and has put a lot of effort into ensuring its effectiveness. To some extent, its approach reflects its own corporate focus and its culture; but most of BT's concerns are those of other companies. In particular, developments like the new Guidelines for Corporate Community Investment, and the measuring techniques produced by the London Benchmarking Group, make it likely that companies such as BT will increasingly seek to explain their community programme by what it achieves, rather than by how much the company puts into it – in other words, outputs rather than inputs. They will also value the relevance of their community programmes to their business, using stakeholder surveys or other methods to ensure an accurate focus. The derived value for the company could be as a required part of the 'total quality' approach to business, as a contributing factor for corporate reputation among customers and public policy makers, or as a valued encouragement for employees. This is not just a matter of good practice: leading businesses do have ethics, they are concerned about their role in society, and benefits flow both ways in a mature relationship with the charitable sector.

CHAPTER FIFTEEN

Whitbread: resource transfer in action

Ian Anderson

Introduction

The transition from paternalistic company philanthropy to Corporate Community Involvement (CCI), in which specific benefits to both sectors are identified, has brought radical changes to the relationship between organisations (both public and private) and the communities in which they operate and of which they are a part. Up until the 1980s the accepted means of supporting the community was to provide charitable donations for non-specific purposes. As far as Whitbread and a number of other businesses were concerned, 1981 changed that approach: events such as the Brixton riots provided a graphic and frightening example of what society might be like if government were left to cope with those problems on its own. It was no accident that Business in the Community (BitC) was founded in that year, and, in a parallel initiative, Whitbread set up a dedicated community team with direct responsibility to its main board.

The next ten years proved a time for learning: businesses struggled to understand their respective role in the community, and community organisations (overcoming initial suspicions) learnt how to harness this new resource for community benefit. Partnerships blossomed with schools, small businesses and voluntary organisations, particularly those involved with issues such as youth exclusion and crime prevention. These partnerships were largely of a financial kind, although some personnel assistance was given.

A year of sharp change in CCI followed in 1991, as certain organisations recognised a huge additional resource that could be made available to the community – their employees.

Encouraging employee volunteering

Many employees had of course already been volunteering as individuals, but what was missing was the support and encouragement of, and recognition from, their employers. To change this, a model was followed that originated in the US, where most corporations recognised the value that their employees could bring to local communities. Volunteering was, and still is today, more ingrained in US culture, stretching back to the pioneering days when giving voluntary assistance was vital, standard practice and often life-saving.

In May 1991, BitC, the Volunteer Centre UK (now the National Centre for Volunteering) and Whitbread launched the Employees in the Community Initiative. Eight companies joined the leadership team, and a guide to employee volunteering was published. The initial scale of these developments was exemplified by the number of entrants to the Whitbread-sponsored award for companies that encouraged their employees to volunteer. In the first year there were a mere five entries, but a swift acceleration followed, and the 1996 award generated over 300 entries.

Whitbread's initial support for employee volunteers concentrated on its larger sites, where 100 or more staff were working. Having communicated the purpose of the initiative to local management, staff were then encouraged to set up small committees to examine how they could assist their local communities. Some projects emanated from the staff, some in response to requests from local organisations, and some came through links with the local volunteer bureau. Committees were encouraged to become involved in hands-on activity, in addition to fundraising, and this was generally considered more satisfying by those involved. Whitbread supplied a dedicated manager, charitable funds to be used locally at the discretion of the volunteers, some company time and facilities, and, crucially, it provided various forms of recognition, including an annual event hosted by the Chairman and the board. Forty-six committees now operate across the UK, each with a small dedicated team, but with the ability to mobilise much larger numbers, depending on the size of projects undertaken. Here are two examples of such activity:

- Thresher staff at the Whitbread distribution centre in Huyton, Liverpool, organise fundraising events throughout the year to raise money to entertain 100 chronically ill children for a Christmas day out at Manchester Airport, including a flight to meet Santa.
- The brewery staff at Magor in Wales heard that a recently disabled man could not enjoy his garden, which was on a slope. The garden was levelled and flower beds placed at wheel-chair height.

The Whitbread business includes many sites with too few members of staff to form committees – for example Thresher, Pizza Hut, Café Rouge – but volunteers in these outlets are encouraged and recognised by the Whitbread Award for Volunteer Effort (WAVE). As long as individuals show a commitment to volunteering by fundraising or giving up time, then they are eligible for an annual award of £200 for the organisation they are supporting. These awards are available to employees and pensioners.

Additional benefits to company and staff

An unexpected side-effect from the encouragement of employee volunteers has been the development of staff, both as individuals and in groups. Management observed positive changes in areas such as confidence, team work, communications and presentation skills. Pilot programmes were set up to test whether structured training using community projects could replicate these benefits.

Team building in Whitbread had traditionally been tackled by sending groups to remote areas for a weekend to build temporary bridges over streams and perform other non-productive tasks. The process worked, but now groups embark on real community tasks that achieve the same team-building end but involve the completion of a worthwhile project: this activity provides much more personal satisfaction and raises the image of Whitbread in the local community. A recent challenge in Bristol involved all 200 members of the Whitbread Beer Company's sales force completing 12 community tasks identified and organised for them by Community Service Volunteers (CSV). The sales team has insisted on a similar activity for its next sales conference.

Individual development is being tackled by community development assignments. Having identified a personal development need, a not-for-profit organisation, such as BitC, is asked to identify a community project that will meet the individual requirement but also benefit the community. It is planned, executed and evaluated exactly as any other training discipline, but it provides community benefit in addition. For example, a Thresher manager improved his communication skills by completing a project with Hinkley Volunteer Bureau that involved researching sources of funding for training courses. Building on the outcomes from our volunteering experiences, it is expected that community involvement projects will become part of the menu of development opportunities available to Whitbread employees.

The resource of company employees, whether as volunteers or as individuals directed to become involved with the community for developmental purposes, is growing and has already become a potent force in community activity.

Unlocking other company resources

The majority of the leading companies in CCI are now involved in contributing money and people resources. The next objective is to release the myriad other resources that companies can offer. There is, first, the huge bank of skills and experience that companies like Whitbread possess and are prepared to offer to the voluntary sector on an occasional basis. Whitbread offers advice to small businesses across the country, through its support for Enterprise Agencies, and also to young individuals involved with the Prince's Youth Business Trust (PYBT): schools, colleges and universities gain from the business skills available from Whitbread school governors or board members; volunteering organisations benefit from trustee involvement and more general advice. Recent examples have included: the redesign of the kitchen and catering area for a Foyer in Scotland by a Beefeater manager; the use of Whitbread's procurement team to advise on the process of tendering; and Whitbread's logistics expertise, which ensured that the 30,000 meals required by the disabled athletes at the Special Olympics were available at the right times and in the right place. The inevitable widening of the network of contacts through a business involvement should not be underestimated. In some cases, our contacts have provided very large financial savings to organisations in the voluntary sector.

Space in and around buildings will sometimes become surplus to an organisation's needs. This may be short term – as in the case of Costa Coffee, where a two-year end-of-lease situation is enabling a homeless centre to offer training space in central London – or longer term – as in the case of the Griffin Hotel in Salford, where three floors above a pub have been converted into 27 small workshops for start-up businesses. Pub car parks can be made available for mobile libraries, and in one case a country pub's disused stable block was converted into a sub post office. Offices in city centres are frequently 'loaned' to voluntary agencies for meetings, and in some cases semi-permanent accommodation can be made available.

Reassigning resources

By far the biggest opportunity in the 'other' resources area is for companies to identify all those items that they no longer need and which, despite being in good condition, would normally be consigned to the scrap heap. Until now Whitbread has adopted a policy of trying to supply individual items requested from time to time by community organisations: a table and chairs, a computer, some carpeting – in other words, by reacting to community needs. In 1997, it decided to trial a pro-active approach and began by piloting a community resources project in its Hotels division.

Marriott Hotels and Travel Inns account for almost 250 hotels and over 16,000 rooms in the UK and, importantly for this project, have a rolling refurbishment programme. From the hotels' point of view, a critical factor in refurbishment is how quickly the individual rooms can be brought back into service, and hitherto unwanted items would be disposed of by the contractor. Not any more – now the details of refurbishments are forwarded as they are being planned to the Community Investment Programme, which then plans their 'second life'. Beds, carpets, wardrobes, curtains, sofas, chairs and mirrors are entered on the resources database and matched with the needs of community organisations held on file. The organisations are then invited to collect the goods as soon as the refurbishment commences. When the Luton Foyer was in its planning stage, the organisers approached Whitbread for help; one of the ways in which the company assisted was by agreeing to furnish the 89 bedrooms on and off site linked to the project. The refurbishment of the Tudor Park Marriott Hotel in Kent coincided on dates, and all 89 bedrooms were furnished, together with most of the common areas of the Foyer. The organisers estimated that Whitbread had saved them in the region of £100,000.

Activities such as this have encouraged Whitbread to develop the concept across the whole of its business, and a full time co-ordinator has been appointed to manage the operation. The community opportunity in a company such as Whitbread is enormous. It can examine items no longer required in restaurants, leisure centres, pubs, offices, breweries, hotels, shops and even children's play areas; the potential for community benefit that could be achieved if all businesses adopted a proactive stance to surplus requirements would be immeasurable.

Beyond financial donations

The provision of financial donations to the community by business will always be important, but will always be of a limited nature. Donations of gifts in time and gifts in kind can add so much to the fabric of the community and can play to the strengths of commercial organisations by using all their resources.

CHAPTER SIXTEEN

Developing a flagship charity campaign

Karen Johnson

Introduction

Nationwide Building Society has had a long tradition of supporting the local communities from which it has grown, a tradition that has proved valuable both to the community projects and charities it has helped and to Nationwide itself. Community Affairs activities undertaken have proved to be an effective way of bringing Nationwide employees together, developing the skills of individuals and creating some positive PR opportunities.

Nationwide receives many requests for support from charities and organisations every day and uses five main criteria to reach a decision about which local or national projects to support as part of its community affairs strategy:

- a desire to support a good cause
- opportunities for employee involvement
- the number of people who will benefit
- the possibility for PR opportunities
- whether the charity or organisation is based in the UK (as a UK-based building society, Nationwide does not generally support overseas initiatives).

It is important that both charity and commercial organisation understand the other's corporate objectives and are able to work together effectively to achieve these. A successful partnership will involve a degree of philanthropy, but increasingly commercial considerations play an important part in deciding on a charity partner. These considerations include opportunities for branding, improved public profile and media coverage. In the case of cause-related marketing, increased sales would clearly be a priority.

All companies and charities have a product, service or image to sell. The fact that many charities are able to target specific age groups or sectors of the population can lead to mutually beneficial partnerships, since these age groups or sectors often fit companies' marketing plans for targeting a specific message, service or product. The reverse is also true: companies may be able to open up new and potentially profitable networks for their charity partners, for example in the form of a retail branch network.

Finding a central focus for community activities

In 1994, Nationwide decided that a 'flagship' charity campaign would be an excellent way of meeting all the objectives of the community programme and act as a central focus for Nationwide's national and local community activities. A number of stages led Nationwide to choose Macmillan Cancer Relief as its 'flagship' charity partner. Important early considerations included financial stability, a national profile and a good reputation with the general public. It was important to Nationwide that the charity had a good 'fit' with itself in terms of infrastructure, distribution and philosophy. Nationwide employees also needed to be able to relate to the chosen charity, since their involvement was a key part of the fundraising.

Macmillan was able to work with Nationwide to develop a campaign where money raised locally would be spent locally, so that employees and members could see the direct benefits of their support in their community. Macmillan had already developed a tried and tested package of sponsorable and marketable events and had an understanding of a potential sponsor's need for branding, publicity and raising campaign awareness on both a local and national scale.

The campaign was initially developed with a very simple structure. Support was provided centrally from the corporate budget, including sponsorship of a number of high-profile events to encourage widespread employee and customer participation. Initially, support concentrated on a Macmillan Breast Cancer awareness campaign. Nationwide sponsored an information leaflet, which was distributed to GP surgeries, health centres and the Society's branches. This led to Nationwide supporting a national free helpline run by Breast Cancer Care, a sister charity. The helpline has proved very successful and has, with the Society's help, grown rapidly over the last three years.

The first major sponsorship was that of title sponsorship for the Nationwide Macmillan Mile Challenge. The partnership on this project gave Nationwide a good opportunity for media involvement and publicity, along with an excellent means to promote employee and member participation. The campaign was very successful for Macmillan in fundraising terms, and both parties benefited from the publicity the challenge attracted.

Local campaigns aimed at generating local participation

'The world's biggest coffee morning' was identified as a project that would boost the Nationwide campaign and at the same time give employees the chance to invite members and customers into Nationwide branches, thereby enabling a large participation. The problem was that Nationwide was not the title sponsor and therefore could not in the first instance send out its own branded materials for internal use. After some fairly protracted discussions, it was agreed that Nationwide could use specially branded merchandise for internal use, while giving prominence to the title sponsor. Macmillan has always shown a commitment to resolving small difficulties as they arise and to understanding Nationwide's needs as well as its own.

Nationwide worked with Macmillan to develop a fundraising campaign that maintained its impetus throughout the year. In addition to major initiatives, Nationwide sold Macmillan lapel badges through its retail branch network, which provided a steady source of income to help the charity towards its fundraising target.

Although the partnership between the two developed successfully over time, in 1997 Nationwide decided to move away from the idea of having a 'flagship' charity, as it was concerned that both members and employees may become 'tired' of fundraising for one charity only. It is a testament to the strength of the relationship between the two organisations that, in the year when there was no formal arrangement, Nationwide's members and employees raised nearly as much for the charity as in the previous year. When employees were asked if they wanted to renew the formal arrangement in 1998, the result was unanimous. The practical demonstration of the success of the relationship is that, since 1994, Nationwide employees and members have raised over £1.8 million for Macmillan. Indeed, in 1999 the relationship was further enhanced by an innovative partnership whereby the benefits of Nationwide's sponsorship of the Football Conference's Challenge Trophy were donated to Macmillan and the trophy itself was named the Nationwide Macmillan Trophy.

The relationship has not always been plain sailing, although both parties are committed to making it an effective one. An issue that arose on a number of occasions in the early days of the relationship was that of sponsor acknowledgement. Some charitable organisations do not fully understand the importance of this for commercial organisations, but Macmillan quickly came to understand the need and now makes a considerable effort to accommodate branding.

Conclusion

So why aren't all commercial companies' relationships with charities as successful as this? It is often the simplest things that build or destroy relationships. Some time ago, a representative from Nationwide visited a charity for a presentation about the charity's work, as a result of which a fairly substantial donation was made. Twelve months later, the charity approached Nationwide for a further donation, but got both the company and addressee details wrong. The impression that this gave was not very favourable and, although it was not the only factor in Nationwide's decision to decline the application, it left a feeling that the previous money had not been appreciated or was not significant enough to the charity to make it want to take the time or effort to build a future relationship.

Charities should be prepared to research the types of projects companies actually support by referring to one of the many funding guides available or by speaking to someone who works in the community support area of the organisation they are approaching. There has been much publicity over the last few years about Nationwide's position as a committed mutual building society. Letters that are addressed to Nationwide Bank do not get a request for support off to a good start, as they show a sloppy approach and suggest they are simply a part of an ill-researched bulk mailing.

Nationwide's experience has shown that it is possible to have an effective relationship with a charity partner that benefits both partners equally. However, it is essential that there is a clear understanding of both parties' expectations and desires. In addition, honesty and a commitment to making the partnership work through good relationship management and through solving problems as they arise, together with the flexibility to adapt, are paramount. It is only when all these vital components are in place that maximum benefit will be gained.

Conclusion

Valerie Morton

Introduction

It is easy to be left with a sense of irony after reading this book. In the decades before the 1980s, as Chapter 1 indicated, corporate fundraising was carried out in a very integrated fashion, on a needs-led basis, involving a very personalised (and usually face-to-face) approach, in many cases involving gifts in kind. The 1980s and early 1990s saw corporate fundraising become a very specialist area, with clear financial targets: some of the case histories in this book (eg, those from the Royal National Institute for the Blind and the Muscular Dystrophy Group) demonstrate this very effectively. Unfortunately, however, the good management practices set out in the first section of the book have not always being adhered to. Blanket approaches are still being used, and despite the good examples of charities (such as that shown by Children's Aid Direct in Chapter 13), gifts in kind are often still considered as poor relations, perhaps because of the difficulty involved in counting them towards financial targets. Things are beginning to change. We are gradually seeing charities realise that companies can have an impact not only on fundraising as a whole but also on the charity as a whole. With regard to fundraising, companies can give money, support direct marketing activity by, for example, distributing appeals with customer mailings, and can benefit community fundraising by supporting volunteering or participation in local events: as shown in Chapter 15, Whitbread has been leading the way in this area. The charity as a whole can benefit through the communication of key messages to the company, its staff and customers, as RNIB's partnership with NFC in Chapter 10 demonstrated. Blanket approaches with scant targeting, although they still take place, are so unlikely to succeed that they must surely die a natural death in the next few years. Gifts in kind are now recognised as the up-and-coming corporate fundraising 'product'.

Into the third millennium

So what trends are likely to be seen in the first decade of the third millennium?

- Following the lead from corporate community affairs departments, charities will need to think more holistically about the support given or generated by companies. Money may be one aspect, but broader support – whether through gifts in kind, providing access to staff and customers, or influence in the community – is likely to increase. Charities will need to adapt their systems and management to ensure they capitalise on the potential.

- As a consequence of the above situation, charities will need to look closely at all the contact points they have with the corporate sector and begin to harmonise approaches. In the 1980s, charities with a number of corporate fundraising staff would more often than not be structured by product specialists. For example, there would be a sponsor manager, donations manager, employee fundraising manager, etc. The recognition that a company, as a customer, needed to be managed effectively resulted in a move towards the 'account management' approach, with each fundraiser having responsibility for certain companies, rather than certain products. Many charities have, or need to develop, corporate contacts in areas other than fundraising. These contacts may be because companies are key target audiences for policy messages, or simply suppliers of goods and services to the charity. The long-standing segregation of functions such as fundraising, finance and administration and service provision will need to be addressed. The winners will be those charities that are capable of bringing about the cultural change this will require.

- Links with Europe, which have been long talked about but, thus far, rarely evidenced, will begin to emerge. More charities will see markets for their services in Europe; more importantly, more companies will give preference to charities that can fulfil their requirements across Europe. As a result, partnerships between UK charities and their European colleagues will develop.

- The voluntary sector will at long last produce very clear guidelines and standards of good practice in corporate fundraising. Fundraisers who continue to send inappropriate, untargeted mailings to companies, who make unrealistic claims concerning the benefits a company will receive from involvement with their charity, who do not understand the key principle of account management, or who fail to deliver on their commitments to a company, will find their luck runs out. The corporate fundraisers who will succeed will be those who combine common sense with good manners, creativity and sound management.

- Someone will devise a truly cost-effective way of raising money from small companies, and there will be fundraisers around who are keen to do the job.
- The impact of devolution in Wales and Scotland will have a significant impact on fundraising partnerships. Companies will expect charities to respond to the wishes of staff and customers by providing localised project branding and contacts.

Undoubtedly, by 2010, things will have changed much more radically than even these predicted developments suggest!

Appendices

Legal and tax issues

Stephen Lloyd

Introduction

This chapter covers legal and tax issues (as they obtained in Autumn 1999) arising from:

- corporate fundraising and donations
- licensing by a charity of its name and/or logo
- sponsorship.

Corporate fundraising and donations

Charities' supporters will give their support in many different ways: some may be prepared to give and expect nothing in return; others may wish to get their staff involved in fundraising as a means of building 'team spirit'; others may want to give via their own charity. All these different methods of giving have potential legal consequences, which charities need to consider.

Legal issues – donations

Charities do not normally have a legal problem in receiving donations. There may be special circumstances when they wish to refuse a donation, but they can do this only when the trustees have reasonable grounds for believing that acceptance of the donation would have an adverse impact on the charity's:

- staff
- volunteers
- supporters
- public image.

However, donations give rise to some tax issues.

Donations and direct tax (Corporation and Income Tax)

Limited companies pay corporation tax on their profits, whereas firms (eg accountants) pay income tax. These are both direct taxes, as opposed to VAT, which is an indirect tax.

If a corporate donor is prepared to make a donation and expects only a minimal acknowledgement, then the gift will be eligible to be treated as a Gift Aid payment. Gift Aid works like this:

(a) The minimum payment must be £250.
(b) The payment must not be subject to any condition as to repayment.
(c) The donor has to complete Form R240(SD) and deduct basic-rate income tax from the donation. The donor has to pay the income tax so deducted to the Inland Revenue, and the charity then reclaims it. It may seem strange for a company that pays corporation tax on its profits rather than income tax to deduct income tax, but that is how the system works.
(d) In the case of 'close companies', the company, or any connected person, must not receive any benefit exceeding 2.5 per cent of the value of the gift but subject to an overall ceiling of £250. A close company is one under the control of five or fewer participators. In the case of a 'non-close company' (eg a company quoted on the Stock Exchange), there is no limit, but Revenue practice seems to vary in treating benefits received by such a donor under Gift Aid. The best advice is to treat all corporate Gift Aid payments as subject to the overall £250 benefit limit.
(e) The donor must be a UK taxpayer.

An example of Gift Aid calculation

XYZ Company makes a Gift Aid payment of £10,000 to ABC Charity.

XYZ will deduct £2,200 (calculated at the current basic rate of income tax of 22 per cent) and pay that to the Inland Revenue. It pays £7,800 to ABC.

ABC recovers £2,200 from the Inland Revenue.

When XYZ computes its taxable profits, the entire £10,000 will be treated as a tax-deductible payment as a charge on income. Many fundraisers think that the Gift Aid rules for companies are the same as they are for individuals and that, if a corporate donor makes a Gift Aid payment, this means that the charity can enhance the size of the gift through the tax relief. From the company's point of view, however, a donation under Gift Aid is just the same as a tax-deductible business expense: both can be offset against profits in calculating its corporation tax liability – the only difference is that, in the case of a donation under Gift Aid, income tax is deducted and paid to the Revenue.

Gift Aid 2000

The Chancellor introduced a new form of giving in the 1998 Budget, targeted at helping the 80 poorest countries in the world. Originally called Millennium Gift Aid, this is now called Gift Aid 2000. It works just like Gift Aid but applies to gifts over £100 (as opposed to gifts over £250). It will run only until 31 December 2000.

Payments have to be made to a qualifying charity, which is one that is registered with the Revenue for these purposes and fulfils the requirements by virtue of the work that it undertakes.

Deeds of covenant

Many corporate supporters prefer the flexibility of making a one-off gift via Gift Aid to committing themselves to the minimum four-year period required by a Deed of Covenant. Charities need to ensure that the Deed complies with the requirements of the Taxes Act 1988. Deeds of Covenant are strictly interpreted and any errors will normally be construed to the Revenue's advantage. It is therefore essential that a charity that is accepting a donation via a deed of covenant should take professional advice. In particular the Deed must:

- show the full name and registered office of the donor;
- be executed as a deed by the donor – in the case of a company, this means that it has been signed by two directors or one director and the company secretary;
- be in a form that has been drafted by a professional or conforms to the Inland Revenue's recommended model;
- be capable of exceeding three years.

If the Deed is defective, do not bank any cheque paid but return the Deed to the donor and have it amended before the cheque is presented. Particular care needs to be taken at the end of the donor's financial year end as the payment has to have been made and the cheque cleared before the end of the financial period if the covenanted donation is to be treated as a charge on income for that year.

As far as the tax system is concerned, Deeds of Covenant are treated like Gift Aid. The donor deducts income tax and pays it to the Inland Revenue, and the charity recovers it. The form used is an R185 (AP).

The disadvantage with a Deed of Covenant, from a charity's point of view, is cash flow, as the gift is spread over a minimum of four years. Sometimes donors can be persuaded to lend all the sums due under a four-year covenant in the first year; this used to be popular before Gift Aid was introduced but is much less so today, for obvious reasons. If the donor is able to afford to part with the entire donation in Year 1, why bother with the complications of a deed and a loan when a one-off Gift Aid payment can be made?

Partnerships

The examples above have been based on the donor being a company. The position is different in the case of partnerships. Partnerships are unincorporated businesses, and each partner is liable for his or her own tax bill. Consequently, when it comes to seeking donations from partnerships, a charity will have to persuade each individual partner to complete the relevant documentation in his or her name. This can be a tall order where there are over one hundred partners in a firm, as is the case with many modern firms. In some cases, the firms may have established their own charity, which will already have received payments under Gift Aid or Deed of Covenant from the partners, and the firm charity will make the donation. To the disappointment of some fundraisers this means that no further tax repayments can be obtained from the Inland Revenue, as a charity cannot itself make a payment under Gift Aid, since it is exempt from UK tax.

It must be emphasised that all these concessions on gifts to charities are subject to the condition that the donor gets no material benefit in return. A small acknowledgement in an annual report or on a programme will not constitute a benefit; but more tangible recognition (eg display of the corporate supporter's logo on the annual report) will. If a charity wishes to do this it should consider making a reasonable charge to the supporter for the display of the supporter's logo: this charge will also attract VAT (see below).

Donations and VAT

Donations and legacies are outside the scope of VAT, even if the donor receives some minor benefit (eg a flag), but, as the Customs & Excise pamphlet on Sponsorship (701/41/95) makes clear:

> to be treated as outside the scope of VAT, the sponsor's support must be entirely voluntary and secure nothing in return. A taxable supply will not be created by the simple acknowledgement of support such as:
>
> (a) giving a flag or sticker,
> (b) inclusion in a list of supporters in a programme, or on a notice,
> (c) naming a building or university chair after the donor
> (d) putting the donor's name on the back of a seat in a theatre.

However, as the pamphlet also makes clear, if a donor makes it a condition that his or her logo or trading name is to be displayed or that he or she is to receive some other benefit, then Customs will treat the entire payment as the consideration for a taxable supply, and the charity will have to account for tax on it.

Examples of Vatable supplies include:

- naming an event after the sponsor
- display of the sponsor's name, logo or trading name
- free or reduced entry
- priority booking rights.

Many charities do display supporter's logos and are not challenged by Customs, but this cannot be regarded as a safe practice in the light of the very clear guidance quoted above. There is one major exception to this rule – where the sponsorship is part of a one-off fundraising event, the sponsorship income is treated as exempt from VAT.

Staff fundraising

Many corporate supporters now wish to involve their staff in fundraising for the company's 'Charity of the Year'. This support can raise a number of issues, as the following example will illustrate.

XYZ Company agrees to encourage its staff members to raise money through a sponsored swimathon for ABC Charity. The staff do this in their own time and solicit donations from the general public. The individual members of staff pay the money they have collected direct to ABC's bank account.

In this case, all that XYZ has done is to encourage staff fundraising and nothing more. Nonetheless, there will be issues that the charity should be aware of in terms of controls on fundraising:

- Are the members of staff fit and proper persons to fundraise for the charity?
- Has the employer warranted that they are?
- Does the charity warn the members of staff of the controls on house-to-house collections if they are going around seeking sponsorship?
- Are the fundraisers being paid any expenses or obtaining benefits worth more than £5 per day or £500 per annum?

In terms of taxation:

- Will the charity be selling merchandise in connection with the event (eg T-shirts, baseball caps, etc)?
- If so, is this being done through the charity or its trading company?
- Should VAT be charged on the items sold?

In terms of risk:

- Who will be organising the event?

- Does the charity need to consider health and safety, risk and liability issues?
- If so, is there adequate insurance cover for all normal risks?
- If not, is there an agreement with the event organiser dealing with these issues?

What is the position where the corporate supporter wants to take a more pro-active role, for example to advertise the fact that ABC Charity is its Charity of the Year throughout its stores? Will this be taken to mean that XYZ is thereby advertising its support? Provided the wording of the advertisements makes it clear that XYZ is facilitating fundraising and nothing else, and that XYZ is paying none of its own money to ABC, there will not be a taxation problem. However, there may be issues under the Charities Act 1992 (see below).

Licences and Charity Law

Cause-related marketing

Cause-related marketing arrangements involve charities licensing their names and/or logos to commercial partners. The name and/or logo is displayed on the commercial partner's goods or on brochures and advertisements advertising its services. The commercial partner in these circumstances is defined under the Charities Act 1992 as a 'commercial participator'. In essence, a commercial participator is someone who encourages purchases of goods or services on the grounds that some of the proceeds will go to a charitable institution or that a donation will be made.

Section 58(1) Charities Act 1992 defines a commercial participator as 'In relation to any charitable institution...any person who: (a) carries on for gain any business other than a fundraising business, but (b) in the course of that business, engages in any promotional venture in the course of which it is represented that charitable contributions are to be given to or applied for the benefit of the institution.'

A number of the expressions used in this definition are also defined in the Act. 'Promotional venture' is defined as any 'Advertising or sales campaign or any other venture undertaken for commercial purposes'. The Oxford English Dictionary defines a venture as 'that which is ventured or risked in a commercial enterprise or speculation'.

'Charitable contributions' is defined as meaning:

> In relation to any representation made by any commercial participator or other person … (a) the whole or part of (i) the consideration given for goods or services sold or supplied by him, or (ii) any proceeds (other than

such consideration) of a promotional venture undertaken by him, or (b) sums given by him by way of donations in connection with the sale or supply of any such goods or services (whether the amount of such sums is determined by reference to the value of such goods or services or otherwise).

Examples of commercial participators include: banks issuing affinity cards in partnership with charities; food companies who sell products with the charity's name and logo on the product stating '5p per packet will go to XYZ Charity'; a travel company that offers to pay 1 per cent of the price of a holiday to a named charity.

Under the Charities Act the commercial participator must have an agreement with what is called a charitable institution (normally a charity).

The agreement between the charitable institution and the commercial participator required by section 59(2) of the 1992 Act has to be in writing and signed by or on behalf of the charitable institution and the commercial participator.

The agreement has to specify:

- the name and address of each of the parties to the agreement;
- the date on which the agreement was signed by or on behalf of each of those parties;
- the period for which the agreement is to subsist;
- any terms relating to the termination of the agreement prior to the date on which that period expires;
- any terms relating to the variation of the agreement during that period.

The agreement also has to contain:

(a) a statement of its principal objectives and the methods to be used in pursuit of those objectives;
(b) provision as to the manner in which are to be determined:
    (i) if there is more than one charitable institution party to the agreement, the proportion in which the institutions which are so party are respectively to benefit under the agreement;
    (ii) the proportion of the consideration given for goods or services sold or supplied by the commercial participator or of any other proceeds of a promotional venture undertaken by him, which is to be given to or applied for the benefit of the charitable institution; or
    (iii) the sums by way of donations by the commercial participator in connection with the sale or supply of any goods or services sold or supplied by him which are to be so given or applied;

as the case may require;

(c) provision as to any amount by way of remuneration or expenses which the commercial participator is to be entitled to receive in respect of things done by him in pursuance of the agreement and the manner in which any such amount is to be determined.

These requirements are the various legal minimums. Charities should also consider whether or not there are other clauses that should be inserted in such a contract to cover their positions. In particular, charities should consider the fact that licensing their name to a commercial organisation can give rise to a number of problems.

Problems of association

Each charity that enters into arrangements whereby its name is to be associated with the goods and/or services provided by a third party needs to appreciate that there is a risk that the charity's name could be brought into disrepute through the activities of the licensee or some member of its group of companies. Modern transnational companies have tentacles spread throughout many countries. The company with which a charity has a licensing arrangement in the UK may be involved in many different industries in many parts of the world, and it is impossible for the charity to check adequately on the performance of all those companies prior to entering into any licence.

Nothing can be 100 per cent watertight in these circumstances, and charities need to proceed with considerable caution. It is therefore suggested that, where a charity is licensing its name, in addition to the requirements laid down under the Charities Act, a charity should request that the contract contain clauses such as:

(a) a minimum guaranteed sum payable to the charity;

(b) a warranty by the licensee that neither it nor any of its associated companies (ie subsidiaries or joint ventures) will at any time during the duration of the agreement do anything that could bring the reputation of the charity into disrepute;

(c) a termination clause allowing the charity to terminate the licence immediately should, in its reasonable opinion, its name be brought into disrepute by the licensee or its associates or if the licensee is in a material breach of any of the terms of the agreement;

(d) a term relating to what happens to stock bearing the charity's logo in the event of early termination of the agreement due to its breach by the licensee;

(e) strict controls on the use of the charity's name and logo and recognition of its copyright;

(f) mutual clearance of all publicity materials and agreed wording to describe each partner and their relationship;

(g) an undertaking that the commercial participator will abide at all times with all relevant health, environmental and legal obligation and codes of best practice;

(h) interest on late payments.

A charity might also wish to seek other clauses such as:

- an agreement that the commercial participator will not enter into a similar arrangement with any other organisation operating in the same field as the charity for the duration of the agreement;
- an indemnity in respect of any losses or damage suffered by the charity as a result of any action by the commercial participator;
- an obligation on the commercial participator to segregate moneys due to the charitable institution in a separate bank account preferably marked with the name of the charity so that, should the commercial participator go into liquidation, the moneys in the account will be deemed to be trust moneys and not part of the general assets of the commercial participator available for distribution to the general body of its creditors.

Section 60(3) provides that, where any representation is made by a commercial participator to the effect that charitable contributions are to be given to or applied for the benefit of one or more particular charitable institution, the representation shall be accompanied by a statement clearly indicating:

(a) the name or names of the institution or institutions concerned;

(b) if there is more than one institution concerned, the proportions in which the institutions are respectively to benefit; and

(c) (in general terms), the method by which it is to be determined

(i) what proportion of the consideration given for goods or services sold or supplied by him, or of any other proceeds of a promotional venture undertaken by him, is to be given to or applied for the benefit of the institution or institutions concerned; or

(ii) what sums by way of donations by him in connection with the sale or supply of any such goods or services are to be so given or applied,

as the case may require.

In almost all cases the statement will be made on the goods themselves or in brochures or catalogues describing the goods or services or through point of sale advertising.

As can be seen, there are two different ways in which the statement can be made, 'as the case may require'. Unfortunately, section 60(3) is not satisfactorily worded.

The first possible statement

'([I]n general terms) the method by which it is to be determined (i) what proportion of the consideration given, etc' – is, on close analysis, confusing. You do not need a general method to work out a proportion. Charities doing deals with commercial participators are advised to ignore completely the statement 'in general terms the method by which it is to be determined' if possible, and seek to ensure that the statement clearly indicates what proportion of the consideration given for the goods or services sold will be given to the charitable institution concerned.

This view is substantiated by the Home Office in their publication *Charitable Fundraising: Professional and Commercial Involvement* (February, 1995) where, on page 5, it is stated:

> We strongly recommend that in the case of commercial participation ... or similar activities by charitable institutions or their connected companies not subject to Part II, that the exact amount going to charitable institutions is given in the statement, expressed net (ie after deduction of all expenses, costs, etc); for example, 'X% of the purchase price goes to charity Y' or '£X per item sold goes ... etc'. Where this cannot be stated exactly then a reasonable alternative is recommended, such as 'a minimum X% ... etc', or 'it is estimated that X% ... etc' provided this is a reasonable statement to make and meets the requirements of the law in the particular circumstances of the case.

> We recommend that only where no such statement can meaningfully be made should a percentage be expressed as a gross figure. In such a case it is most important that attention is drawn in the statement to the significance of that fact, ie that further expenses will have to be paid, reducing the benefit that the charitable institution will receive from the donation.

Seeking to deal with the problem thrown up by the phrase '(in general terms) the method by which it is to be determined, etc', the Home Office recommendations go beyond the express letter of the law in requiring rather more precise statements. Charities should be wary of agreeing to arrangements whereby they accept ' X per cent of the net profits', as this begs the question 'net of what?' If this formula is to be accepted, charitable institutions need to be very careful and thorough in agreeing what deductions can be made in order to arrive at the net-profit figure: beware of such all-embracing phrases as 'management charges'. However, charities need to be realistic: it is sometimes very difficult for commercial participators to make precise statements as to what proportion of the price paid will go to the charity because of the complexities of particular commercial arrangements. Agreed minimum donations can be very useful in these circumstances.

The second possible statement:

> (to state in general terms) the method by which it is to be determined ... what sums by way of donation by the commercial participator in connection with the sale or supply of such goods are to be given.

The best example of this is where a charity's trading company states that '100 per cent of its taxable profits are paid to XYZ Charity'.

Direct Tax (Corporation and Income Tax)

The surplus or profit that a charity makes from licensing its name and or logo is not derived from carrying out the charity's purposes. A charity cannot be established to license its name and logo as a charitable activity. Licensing is a form of non-charitable trading, and any surplus is therefore liable to be taxed. The crucial points for fundraisers to bear in mind on contracts with commercial participators are as follows.

If the agreement:

- lasts for more than one year,
- and the charity only licenses its name and/or logo,
- and the charity does nothing else, eg co-operating on marketing or licensing its data base,
- and the Inland Revenue accepts that the charity is not trading in its name and logo,

then it is possible for the payment to be made to the charity as what is called an annual payment. You should take professional advice about this; note, too, that, just because the payment is made to the charity, this does not alter the VAT position.

However, many commercial promotions last for less than a year, so that, for example, Charity A's name appears on a brand of cereal for three months. In this case, the annual payment route will not work. To avoid direct tax on any surplus on the profits from the arrangement, therefore, it is necessary to structure it so that payment is made to the charity's trading company. If the charity wishes to provide more services (eg co-operation on marketing or licensing its database), these services must always be put through the charity's trading company and an appropriate charge made.

VAT

Customs and Excise treat the licensing by a charity, or its trading company, of its name and/or logo to a commercial partner as a taxable supply for VAT purposes. As a result, if the charity or trading company is not registered for VAT, and the price charged for the licence will bring it above the VAT registration threshold (£51,000 in 1999), it will be necessary for it to register for VAT. If it is already registered, it will have to charge VAT on the payment made by the commercial participator to the charity or its trading company. This may come as a surprise to fundraisers and the charity's corporate supporter who will regard an on-pack promotion as advertising the corporate partner's support for the charity – but such arguments cut little ice with the VAT people. So far as they are concerned, the arrangement constitutes a payment by the commercial participator to the charity for the right to link its name with the charity's. The charity or trading company will therefore need to be told how much money is to be paid by the commercial participator and then render a VAT invoice for that amount. This can be dealt with in the agreement with the commercial participator.

In the case of affinity cards, Customs and Excise were prepared to give a concession so that 80 per cent of the payment made by the affinity card company is treated as a donation, and only 20 per cent as a payment for the right to use the charity's name and logo on the credit card and in conjunction with the advertising – which is subject to VAT. That payment is made to the charity's trading company. This unique concession applies only to affinity cards and cannot be taken as a rule of thumb for any other commercial licence.

If the commercial participator carries out VAT-exempt supplies (eg banking or financial services), it cannot recover any VAT charged. In such cases, the commercial participator may insist that all payments are VAT inclusive so that the charity has to account for the VAT out of the sum received. It may be possible to split the payment from the commercial participator between a charge for the use of the charity's name and logo, which will attract VAT, and a donation for the rest of the payment, which will be VAT free. Any such split must be commercially justified – in other words, the price charged for the use of the name and logo must be fair and reasonable – and, if you are considering operating such a split, you should take professional advice.

Fundraisers should also be aware that, so long as the commercial participator is registered for VAT, it is usually in the charity's interest to charge VAT, because this will increase the charity's amount of output VAT which should in turn allow the charity to increase its rate of recovery of input VAT.

Sponsorship

Sponsorship is a Janus word: like the Egyptian god, it faces two ways. Sometimes the term merely means to give charitable support, as in the person who sponsors someone else to swim a hundred metres or cycle a thousand kilometres. On the other hand, it can also mean the act of supporting another organisation in return for recognition: the best example of this meaning is the

Premiership Football teams who display their sponsors' logos over television sets all over the globe. The sponsors of charities may be less visible, but the principle is the same: the sponsor is being rewarded for their support; the charity is giving recognition of that support.

Charities and their sponsors need to consider the effects of the Charities Act 1992 on their arrangements (see 'Licences and Charity Law' above). A commercial sponsor may fall within the definition of a 'commercial participator' (see above). Whether or not the sponsor is a 'commercial participator' will depend upon whether or not a sponsorship payment amounts to the 'proceeds...of a promotional venture'. Whether a sponsorship payment is a proceed is a difficult question to answer: it will depend upon the different facts of different arrangements. But if the sponsor requests that the charity agrees to the sponsor advertising their support on the sponsor's goods (eg 'XYZ Corporation is proud to announce that it has given £100,000 to ABC Charity'), then this will certainly make the sponsor a commercial participator.

This will also constitute a licence by ABC Charity to XYZ Corporation of its name, and ABC should consider the points made above about licensing.

Charity law

Quite apart from the impact of the Charities Act 1992, charities that are considering entering into sponsorship deals also need to consider whether they have the appropriate power to do so. For those charities where the sponsorship underpins a primary-purpose activity it will be possible to argue that the charity is facilitating the achievement of its primary purpose. If that is not the case, what is the position? All charities have an express or implied power to carry on one-off fundraising activities, but a continuing sponsorship arrangement that does not underpin a primary purpose cannot be construed as a one-off event. It is a continuing activity that is not in fulfilment of a charity's primary purpose and therefore cannot be undertaken by the charity. To engage in the sponsorship, the charity must establish a separate trading company instead. This in turn means that the charity should consider a number of key issues.

Issues surrounding the establishment of trade companies

The first issue is whether the charity has the power in its constitution to establish a private company and to buy shares in it – many charities have limited investment powers, as laid down by the Trustee Investments Act 1961, which only allows a charity, broadly speaking, to invest in companies that are quoted on the Stock Exchange or in government securities. If this is the case, a charity will need to amend its constitution to enable it to invest in shares in a private company: this will require the consent of the Charity Commission.

The charity will need to be able to justify its reasons for wanting to establish a trading company.

The second issue is whether the charity has a trading company, or, once it has established one, what the relationship should be between the charity and the trading company. It will be unlikely that a sponsorship arrangement will require working capital; but, if it does (eg because a joint marketing campaign needs to be financed), then the charity must abide by the Charity Commission's guidelines on investments in trading companies. Most such investment is by loan. Any loan must:

- not be interest free – interest should be charged at a reasonable and proper rate, based on the premise that the trustees are investing the charity's funds;
- be secured by a charge over the company's assets, even if these are only a stock of outdated Christmas cards;
- provide terms for its repayment – typically such loans are made repayable on demand.

Finally, there should be a contract between the trading company and the charity, setting out in detail their relationship and covering in particular such topics as:

- the price to be paid by the trading company for the use of the charity's assets (eg staff, office premises, databases, etc), normally calculated on an apportionment basis and invoiced monthly or quarterly in arrears;
- a non-exclusive licence from the charity to the trading company of the charity's name and logo, to enable the trading company to enter into licensing arrangements (see below).

The charges that are made by the charity to the trading company must be calculated on an arms-length basis; the charity must not provide the trading company with the right to use its assets at less than market value, as this could jeopardise the donation by the trading company to the charity of its profits, whether under Deed of Covenant or Gift Aid, as those donations must not be tainted by the suggestion of the donor receiving any benefit in return.

VAT

Sponsorship payments will attract VAT, unless they are paid as part of a one-off fundraising event. For most corporate sponsors, this is not a problem: the charity (or its trading company) will render a VAT invoice for the amount of the sponsorship. The sponsor will in most cases have no problem with this, as it is able to recover any input VAT. However, problems do arise where the sponsor carries on exempt supplies (eg financial services or insurance). In these cases, they cannot recover the VAT, so for them VAT is an additional expense which they will be reluctant to incur. Faced with this problem, many sponsors who carry out exempt supplies insist on the charity bearing the VAT. If a sponsorship of £10,000 is treated as VAT inclusive, and the charity has to account for the VAT out of the £10,000, it loses £1,750.

To respond to this, some charities have arranged the relationship as follows:

- The charity and the sponsor agree to divide the sponsorship into two. One payment will be for the advertising services to be granted to the sponsor by the charity. The split must be fair and proper and capable of being justified to Customs & Excise. That payment will attract VAT and, for the reasons set out below, will be paid to the charity's trading company.
- The other payment will be a gift, to be paid to the charity and to be made under Gift Aid.

There should be two documents to regulate this;

(a) An agreement between the trading company and the sponsor to deal with the sponsorship, the licence of the sponsor's trademark and name to the trading company, and the services to be rendered to the sponsor.
(b) A deed between the sponsor and the charity committing the sponsor to make the agreed donation. If the gift is made up front, so that the charity has it at the outset, a deed will be unnecessary; but many of these arrangements provide for the gift to be paid in stages. If so, the commitment must be by deed, as otherwise it is legally unenforceable. A mere promise to pay cannot be enforced unless the promise is made by deed.

Another variant may be suggested by those would-be sponsors who carry on VAT-exempt supplies and who have their own charity, funded by donations from the sponsor (eg the XYZ Company Charitable Trust). It has been known for the sponsor to propose that, because of the VAT issues, the sponsorship payments should come as a form of charitable grant from the XYZ Company Charitable Trust. If the recipient charity ('ABC') merely receives the grant and gives a small acknowledgement in its annual report, there is no problem. But what if the XYZ Company Charitable Trust has the same corporate style as XYZ Company? And what if the XYZ Company Charitable Trust insists that its name and style appear on ABC's notepaper? In these circumstances, it seems clear that ABC is rendering advertising services to the XYZ Company Charitable Trust; consequently, VAT should be charged by ABC on the value of the 'grant'.

Direct tax (corporation and income tax)

The rules relating to sponsorship income and direct tax are far from easy. In the usual sponsorship arrangements, so far as the sponsor is concerned the payment is a tax-deductible business expense. But the position is far more complicated from the charity's point of view. Before analysing the Inland

Revenue rules, it is worth emphasising the point that corporation or income tax are only paid on profits, and it is unlikely that any event or activity that receives sponsorship will yield a surplus on the sponsorship income. Normally there are plenty of expenses to offset against the sponsorship income so as to ensure there is no surplus.

Charities are exempt from taxation on profits if:

- the profits are applied solely for the purposes of the charity and
- either (a) the trade is exercised in the course of the actual carrying out of a primary purpose of the charity (ie the main objects of the charity as set out in the charity's constitution) or (b) the work in connection with the trade is mainly carried out by beneficiaries of the charity (eg the sale of goods produced by disabled people in workshops).

Unfortunately for charities the activity of providing advertising services to sponsors does not fall neatly into the categories of tax-exempt trading. It is not a primary-purpose activity for a charity to provide advertising services in return for a fee.

The Inland Revenue draws a distinction between:

- sponsorship that underwrites or follows a primary purpose and
- sponsorship that is stand-alone trade.

In the case of sponsorship that follows a primary-purpose trade (eg support from a sponsor of a charitable theatre company), the Revenue accepts that any surplus that the charity obtains from the sponsorship deal is tax free, as it is part of the income derived by the charity from carrying on its primary purpose – in this case, operating a charitable theatre.

On the other hand, if the sponsorship does not underwrite a primary-purpose trade, the position is different. For example, a charity that is established to alleviate poverty in developing countries circulates information packs on development issues free of charge to schools. The costs are underwritten by XYZ Company, whose name and logo are given prominent display on the pack. If (and it is a major 'if') the charity makes a surplus on the arrangement, that surplus will be taxable as being income derived from carrying out a non-primary purpose business of providing advertising services.

What is worse, the Revenue also has the capacity to tax *all* the profits of a charity that derive from a mixed primary- and non-primary-purpose trade: in other words, by creating a surplus from sponsorship, a charity could expose its profits from primary-purpose activities to the risk of tax too! This means that charities engaging in sponsorship deals that do not underwrite a primary-purpose trading activity should consider carefully whether that activity should be put through a trading company.

Conclusion

As this chapter shows, different types of corporate fundraising strategies can give rise to different legal and tax consequences, some of them complicated. Charities entering into such arrangements need to understand all the detail involved and subject that detail to proper legal and tax analysis in order to ensure that the arrangements are structured appropriately to minimise the risks. Failure to do this could mean that the charity suffers unnecessary taxation. If that is the case, trustees of a charity could be taken to have acted in breach of their trust and could be sued and ordered to pay the charity the amount that the charity had lost, out of their own pockets, if the case against them were proven. This may sound fanciful, but the Charity Commission is on record as stating that trustees who allow their charities to incur unnecessary tax bills could themselves be personally liable for any loss so suffered. The only way to ensure that arrangements are structured in the most tax-efficient manner is to understand the details from the outset and, if appropriate, take specialist professional advice.

List of useful contacts

Business in the Community
44 Baker Street
London
W1M 1DH
tel: 020 7224 1600

Centre for Interfirm Comparison
32 St Thomas Street
Winchester
Hampshire
SO23 9HJ
tel: 01962 844144

Charities Aid Foundation
Kings Hill
West Malling
Kent
ME19 4TA
tel: 01732 520000

114–118 Southampton Row
London
WC1B 5AA
tel: 020 7400 2300

Charity Commission
Harmonsworth House
13–15 Bouverie Street
London
EC4Y 8DP
tel: 0870 333 0123

2nd Floor
20 Kings Parade
Queen's Dock
Liverpool
L3 4DQ
tel: 0870 333 0123

Woodfield House
Tangier
Taunton
Somerset
TA1 4BL
tel: 0870 333 0123

Corporate Citizen Magazine
Directory of Social Change
24 Stephenson Way
London
NW1 2DP
tel: 020 7209 4422

EIRIS Services Ltd
80–84 Bond Way
London
SW8 1SF
tel: 020 7840 5700

Gifts in Kind (UK)
PO Box 140
20 St Mary at Hill
London
EC3R 8NA
tel: 020 7204 5003

LEA Events
12 St James Square
London
SW1Y 4RB
tel: 020 7379 1133

Institute of Charity Fundraising Managers
Central Office
Market Towers
1 Nine Elms Lane
London
SW8 5NQ
tel: 020 7627 3436

Scottish Business in the Community
115 George Street
Edinburgh
EH2 4JN
tel: 0131 220 3001

References

Adkins S (1999) *Cause Related Marketing: who cares wins.* Oxford: Butterworth-Heinemann.

Business in the Community/Research International (UK) Ltd (1996) *The Winning Game: quantitative Cause Related Marketing research.* London: BitC.

Business in the Community/Research International (UK) Ltd (1997) *The Game Plan: qualitative Cause Related Marketing research.* London: BitC.

Business in the Community/Research International (UK) Ltd (1998) *The Corporate Survey II: quantitative Cause Related Marketing research.* London: BitC.

Byers J (1998) 'Payroll giving' in Pharoah C and Smerdon M (eds) (1998) *Dimensions of the Voluntary Sector.* West Malling: CAF.

Corporate Citizen/Directory of Social Change (1998) 'Corporate Citizen's top 50 corporate fundraising charities, 1997–98', *Corporate Citizen*, Issue 23, Spring/Summer 1998. London: Directory of Social Change.

Dunn and Bradstreet (1999) *Key British Enterprises.* High Wycombe: Dunn and Bradstreet.

Pharoah C (1998) 'CAF's top 500 corporate donors' in Pharoah C and Smerdon M (eds) (1998) *Dimensions of the Voluntary Sector.* West Malling: CAF.

Hemmington Scott Ltd *PricewaterhouseCoopers Corporate Register.* London: Hemmington Scott Ltd.

About CAF

CAF, Charities Aid Foundation, is a registered charity with a unique mission – to increase the substance of charity in the UK and overseas. It provides services that are both charitable and financial which help donors make the most of their giving and charities make the most of their resources.

Many of CAF's publications reflect the organisation's purpose: *Dimensions of the Voluntary Sector* offers the definitive financial overview of the UK voluntary sector, while the *Directory of Grant Making Trusts* provides the most comprehensive source of funding information available.

As an integral part of its activities, CAF works to raise standards of management in voluntary organisations. This includes the making of grants by its own Grants Council, sponsorship of the Charity Annual Report and Accounts Awards, seminars, training courses and the Charities Annual Conference, the largest regular gathering of key people from within the voluntary sector. In addition, Charitynet (www.charitynet.org) is now established as the leading Internet site on voluntary action.

For decades, CAF has led the way in developing tax-effective services to donors, and these are now used by more than 250,000 individuals and 2,000 of the UK's leading companies, who between them give £150 million each year to charity. Many are also using CAF's CharityCard, the world's first debit card designed exclusively for charitable giving. CAF's unique range of investment and administration services for charities includes the CafCash High Interest Cheque Account, two common investment funds for longer-term investment and a full appeals and subscription management service.

CAF's activities are not limited to the UK, however. Increasingly, CAF is looking to apply the same principles and develop similar services internationally, in its drive to increase the substance of charity across the world. CAF has offices and sister organisations in the United States, Bulgaria, South Africa, Russia, India and Brussels.

For more information about CAF, please visit www.CAFonline.org/

Other publications from CAF

The Directory of Grant Making Trusts
16th Edition
ISBN 1–85934–078–4   £89.95 (3 Volumes)

Grant making trusts represent a major source of support for charitable activity in the UK – in 1997 alone they contributed over £1.9 billion. They support a wide variety of causes and their criteria for allocating funds are often very specific. The *Directory of Grant Making Trusts* (*DGMT*) keeps fundraisers in touch with changes in trusts' funding priorities. Its extensive indexing allows great precision in the targeting of trusts – thus reducing the flow of irrelevant applications and saving time and money at both ends.

The information published in the *DGMT* is the result of extensive research and close liaison with the trust community; it provides the most comprehensive picture of UK trusts currently published. As well as listing over 3,500 trusts – of which 1,500 are new to this edition – the directory now features top 10 sample grants for hundreds of trusts and a new index by grant type. With the addition of the new third volume providing detailed commentaries on 250 of the major trusts, the *DGMT* now represents a complete, one-stop information shop for the trust fundraiser.

Grantseeker
The interactive CD-ROM for fundraisers
£58.69 (incl VAT) for each six-monthly release

Drawing on CAF's years of experience as a publisher of the *Directory of Grant Making Trusts*, *Grantseeker* is the tailor-made solution to the information needs of trust fundraisers in the electronic age. Published for the first time as a subscription service, users will receive a completely new updated edition every six months.

Fully interactive, *Grantseeker*'s specially designed search engine will quickly scan the entire *DGMT* database on the basis of a user's own selection criteria and generate a 'hit list' of trusts whose funding preferences match their project or cause. There are two additional search functions: the ability to search on trustees' names and a key word search by town or city which allows users a more closely defined geographical search. Users' bookmarks and notes automatically carry over to each new release.

Taking full advantage of the extra options available via an electronic search tool, *Grantseeker* offers a more sophisticated matching service than can be provided by traditional methods, enabling fundraisers to save weeks of effort and frustration. A simple hypertext link can provide them with a complete *DGMT* entry on a potential funder within moments of loading the CD. The days of ultimate dependence on a paper-based directory are over.

Grantseeker runs under Windows 95 or above.

The CAF/ICFM Fundraising Series

Trust Fundraising
Anthony Clay (editor)
ISBN 1–85934–069–5   £19.95

Grant-making trusts exist solely to give money away and contribute up to one-fifth of the total voluntary income of United Kingdom charities. Yet, fundraisers continue to approach grant-making trusts in a strangely amateur fashion, sending blanket appeals to trustees, and making requests for support for projects that are clearly outside the defined objects of the trust.

This book outlines a variety of approaches to grant-making trusts that will save trustees' time and ensure greater success for fundraisers by emphasising the importance of research, the use of available contacts, and the need for a detailed strategy for trust fundraising.

Fundraising Strategy
Redmond Mullin
ISBN 1-85934-056-3   £14.95

Fundraising today demands a substantial commitment of people, resources and marketing. Rigorous, strategic planning is a prerequisite if a campaign is to achieve success and a viable return on investment. This book aims to clarify the principle and process of strategy and to demonstrate its place in fundraising campaigns.

Legacy Fundraising
Sebastian Wilberforce (editor)
ISBN 1-85934-055-5   £14.95

Legacy fundraising is a specialist activity. Charities need to recognise its unique characteristics and sensitivities and devise a strategy based on detailed research into past and future supporters. This book demonstrates the formulation of such an approach in practice, mixing practical case histories with more theoretical exposition.

About the ICFM

The ICFM was established in 1983 to provide an individual membership body committed to the highest standards in fundraising for not-for-profit organisations and charities. The Institute now has over 3,000 individual members working in or for charities and voluntary organisations in a fundraising capacity. In addition, the Institute's Charitable Trust has over 400 national, regional and local charities and companies affiliated to its aims and objectives.

All members of the Institute agree, as a point of membership, to abide by its Code of Conduct and various Codes of Practice and Guidance Notes. The Institute administers a structured three-tier training programme covering all aspects of fundraising technique and management. Individual members of the Institute receive the *Update* newsletter, keeping them abreast of changes in work practice and amendments to law at national and international level. Through its eleven regional groups, individual members of the Institute have the opportunity to meet other fundraisers operating in their own locality, to discuss issues of common concern and to participate in training programmes and in the policy development of the ICFM as a whole.

Each year the Institute manages the National Fundraising Convention, the major annual focus for fundraising activity in the United Kingdom, held over three days in the Birmingham area.

The ICFM is recognised by government, the Charity Commission and, increasingly, throughout the voluntary sector as the lead body in providing self-regulation in fundraising practice. This process is managed through compliance with the Code of Conduct and through the development of a range of Codes of Practice covering specific fundraising techniques and designed to provide clear guidance to practising fundraisers on what is efficient, effective and, above all, appropriate practice.

The ICFM promotes research into existing and developing fundraising techniques, and provides a central base for information and data on fundraising held in its library at its national offices in London.

Any individual or charity actively fundraising is eligible to apply for either individual membership or corporate affiliation of the ICFM.

Other publications from the ICFM

Published codes of practice

	Member	Non-member
Code of Practice on Reciprocal Mailing	£1.25	£2.50
Code of Practice on Schools	£1.25	£2.50
Code of Practice on Telephone Recruitment of Collectors	£1.25	£2.50
The Scottish Code of Fundraising Practice	£5.00	£10.00
The Use of Chain Letters	£1.25	£2.50
Static Collection Boxes	£1.25	£2.50
Outbound Telephone Support	£1.25	£2.50
House to House Collections	£1.25	£2.50
Acceptance/Refusal of Donations	£1.25	£2.50
Code of Practice on Outdooor Events	£1.25	£2.50
Consultants Group Code of Practice	FREE	FREE
Code of Practice on Legacies	£1.25	£2.50

Published books

The Complete Fundraising Handbook *Sam Clark*	£13.95	£14.95
Charity Appeals: the complete guide to success *Marion Allford*	£13.59	£15.99
Writing Better Fundraising Applications *Michael Norton*	£9.95	£12.95
Who's Who in Fundraising	£10.00	£20.00
Schools Fundraising *Ann Mountfield*	£10.50	£12.95
Fundraising on the Internet *Howard Lake*	£10.50	£12.95
Handbook of Fundraising Consultancy	£6.00	£12.00
Reference Manual on Payroll Giving	FREE	£2.50

To order any of the above publications, please contact:

ICFM, Central Office, Market Towers, 1 Nine Elms Lane, London SW8 5NQ
Telephone 020 7627 3436/020 7978 2761

Index